SPINOZA
the outcast thinker

**PHILOSOPHY FOR
YOUNG PEOPLE**

E. HADER pinxit.   1885   Gesetzlich geschützt.

B. de Spinoza

Phot. u. Verl. v. Sophus Williams, Berlin W.

SPINOZA

the outcast thinker

DEVRA LEHMANN

PHILOSOPHY FOR YOUNG PEOPLE

SEVEN STORIES PRESS
New York • Oakland • London

A TRIANGLE SQUARE BOOK FOR YOUNG READERS
PUBLISHED BY SEVEN STORIES PRESS

Text copyright © 2014, 2024 by Devra Lehmann

SEVEN STORIES PRESS
140 Watts Street
New York, NY 10013
www.sevenstories.com

Teachers may order free
examination copies of Seven Stories Press titles.
Visit https://www.sevenstories.com/pg/resources-academics
or email academic@sevenstories.com.

Library of Congress Cataloging-in-Publication Data

Names: Lehmann, Devra, author.
Title: Spinoza : the outcast thinker / Devra Lehmann.
Description: New York, NY : Seven Stories Press, [2024] | Includes
bibliographical references and index. | Audience: Ages 13-17 years |
Audience: Grades 10-12
Identifiers: LCCN 2023037993 | ISBN 9781644212622 (trade paperback) | ISBN
9781644212639 (ebook)
Subjects: LCSH: Spinoza, Benedictus de, 1632-1677. |
Philosophers--Netherlands--Biography. | CYAC: Biographies. lcgft
Classification: LCC B3997 .L44 2023 | DDC 199/.492--dc23/eng/20231130
LC record available at https://lccn.loc.gov/2023037993

Book design by Stewart Cauley and Beth Kessler

Printed in the USA

9 8 7 6 5 4 3 2 1

For Ron

Contents

Preface

I BELIEVE THAT I FIRST HEARD ABOUT SPINOZA IN A
Jewish history class taught by an elderly
gentleman named Armin Steif. The setting was
an Orthodox Jewish girls' high school, hardly
the place for an extensive discussion of Spinoza's
ideas, and I remember Mr. Steif quickly working
through the topic as we covered the aftermath of
the Spanish Inquisition. I realized far too late that
Mr. Steif was a highly cultured and reflective man,
and today the memory of his vivid eyes sometimes
haunts me. I wonder what he would say to me now
if I could show him this book. In the context of
his class and in the setting of that school, he said
only that Spinoza was a very smart Jew tragically
gone "off the path"—certainly enough information
to pique the interest of a teenager with lots of big
questions.

That interest lay dormant for many years. The philosophy courses I took in college did not feature Spinoza, who was not as popular then as he is today, and my studies carried me off in different directions. My curiosity revived only when my friend Tirosh Feldman recommended Jonathan Israel's *Radical Enlightenment*, which takes as its thesis Spinoza's centrality in ushering in our modern world. About a quarter of the way through the book, I realized that I needed to set it aside temporarily. I did not know enough about Spinoza himself.

Two other friends, Meir Ekstein and Jeremy Cohen, provided me with helpful material and an excellent reading list, and my odyssey began. At first, it was purely a personal inquiry aimed at filling a huge gap in my own knowledge. But I have been a teacher for a very long time, and I could not forget myself as a student in Mr. Steif's class. So I naturally began working on this book.

Many other friends and acquaintances helped along the way, including Gadi Haber, Carmi Horowitz, Esther Krauss, Onnie Schiffmiller, Miriam Zussman, Paia Ehrenwald, Ira Miller, Sharon Grossman, Anna Olswanger, Norman Finkelstein, Liz Seymour, Ilana Kurshan, and Roberta Israeloff. Steven Nadler, Professor of

Philosophy at the University of Wisconsin–Madison and a prominent scholar on Spinoza, graciously looked over my draft. Hindy Lederman shot my author photo, and Colin Alexander helped with the maps.

Colin also painted the beautiful image that appeared on the original cover. *Spinoza: The Outcast Thinker* was first published in 2014 by namelos, where my editor, Karen Klockner, showed a consistent combination of expertise and kindness. I am delighted that Seven Stories is now reissuing this book as part of Philosophy for Young People. I thank Oona Holahan for editing with intelligence, enthusiasm, and organization and Stewart Cauley for giving this edition a lively new design.

Finally, my family deserves recognition for supporting me in incalculable ways. We are no longer quite the same group that we were when I first wrote this book, but my gratitude to my parents, Haia Goldenberg and Asher Wolfe, remains unchanged, and I still chuckle at how my children, Danny, Ariella, J.J., and Noam, tolerated a mother distracted by a phantom presence that they waggishly nicknamed "Spinny." Since then, we have been joined by members big and small: Roni, Matanel, Naama, Omer, Eyal, Arbel, Nehara, and

Aluma. All of you have enriched my life with your love, wonder, and humor.

And, as ever, there is my husband, Ron. As Amy Lowell wrote of a partnership mellowed over many years, "I am completely nourished."

PART ONE

A Jew in Amsterdam

PROLOGUE

JULY 27, 1656, WAS A DAY OF HORROR, ANGER, AND
sadness: the Jewish community of Amsterdam
had gathered to cast off one of its own members.
This was not a matter to be taken lightly. The
community was a large but intimate family forged
by long years of suffering—and, more recently, by
years of thankful celebration. In the several blocks
of the city that the Jews called their home, everyone
knew everyone else, and the connections frequently
stretched back several generations.

The crowd was somber as it waited with nervous
anticipation inside the main synagogue. Friends
and neighbors acknowledged each other's presence,
but greetings were muted. The light, too, was
muted. In a sign of mourning, the only sources of
illumination were the black candles held by some of
the congregants.

For some of those gathered in the synagogue, the mere thought of the individual to be expelled aroused a righteous fury. Others felt only a leaden despair. But if the Jewish community was a body, one of its limbs had become incurably infected. The only solution was to cut it off.

The muted conversations ceased as an official of the community mounted the *bima*, the raised platform in the middle of the sanctuary from which the Torah, the holy scroll containing the Five Books of Moses, was normally chanted. Reading from a prepared document in a formal, legalistic style, the official briefly laid out the facts of the case. The offender had adopted evil opinions and had committed monstrous deeds. The offender had persisted in his abominations despite the community's many efforts to reform him. The offender, in consequence, was being cast from the Jewish people for all eternity.

Relatives, friends, and neighbors of the offender held their breath as a long and furious series of curses rang ominously through the sanctuary. Each curse was another toll of the death bell:

> *Cursed be he by day and cursed be he by night; cursed be he when he lies down and cursed be he when he rises up. Cursed be he when he goes out and cursed be he when he comes in. The*

*Lord will not spare him, but then the anger of
the Lord and his jealousy shall smoke against
that man, and all the curses that are written in
this book shall lie upon him, and the Lord shall
blot out his name from under heaven. And the
Lord shall separate him unto evil out of all the
tribes of Israel, according to all the curses of the
covenant that are written in this book of the
law.*

The members of the crowd gasped. The
community had dealt with offenders before, but
such fury was unprecedented. And now they were
to hear what all this meant in terms of daily life.
Still on the platform, the official spelled out the
rules. No Jew—including even the offender's closest
relatives—was to have any further contact with
the offender whatsoever. It was forbidden to speak
with him, to communicate in writing with him,
to read any texts he had written or might write in
the future. It was even forbidden to remain under
the same roof that sheltered him or to approach
within four cubits—about six to eight feet—of his
presence. If the symbolism of these measures was
not sufficiently clear, the snuffing out of the black
candles now made it unmistakable: the offender was
dead to the community in which he had spent his
entire life.

The Jews of Amsterdam had been moved to this drastic step by an outrage that would soon spread throughout Europe. It would not be long before Bento de Spinoza, the individual at the center of the scandal, would be labeled the most dangerous and impious man of the century. Some people even considered him the devil himself, a hideous creature who had forged his ideas in hell in order to drag everyone else down with him to eternal damnation.

CHAPTER I

PERSECUTION IN SPAIN AND PORTUGAL

TWENTY-THREE YEARS EARLIER, THE FEARSOME scene in the synagogue was beyond anyone's wildest imaginings. When Spinoza's parents, Michael and Hanna, held their son for the first time, they felt only a deep sense of blessing. The date was November 24, 1632, and in just eight days their newborn boy would be circumcised according to Jewish tradition. As part of that ceremony, the child would symbolically become a member of the Jewish people and be given his Hebrew name.

Michael and Hanna did not take for granted their ability to celebrate these Jewish traditions. At the time, Jews were not allowed to live, let alone practice their religion, in many other places in Europe. But the Spinozas' new home, the city of Amsterdam, was different. It was already gaining a reputation as the most tolerant city in Europe, a place where people with different religious views could live in safety. Michael had been born in Portugal, where people who practiced Judaism often paid with their lives.

How the newborn baby's family made its way from Portugal to Amsterdam is a story that begins many years earlier in Spain. For well over a thousand years, Jews had lived in Spain, where they had contributed actively to their homeland's cultural and economic life and had been relatively free to lead their lives as they saw fit. They had had a particularly good relationship with the Muslim rulers of Spain during the Middle Ages.

But by the late 1300s and early 1400s, much of Spain had been taken over by Christians, and Jews frequently became the victims of intolerant Christian mobs. Large numbers of Jews were killed or sold as slaves, while others were forced to convert to Christianity. Many of these converted Jews developed a commitment to their new religion, but a significant group began to lead a double life. To the outside world they presented themselves as Christians, but, within their hearts and minds, they identified themselves as Jews. These forced converts to Christianity did their best to follow Jewish practices in secret. But because these secret Jews, or crypto-Jews, were now officially Christian, their attempt to keep their own traditions alive was considered a terrible sin. More specifically, the sin was heresy, the refusal to believe or act as one's religion demands. New Christians who were suspected of secretly practicing Judaism became known by the insulting term *marranos*, meaning "swine" in Spanish, and they faced the constant suspicion of their Old Christian neighbors. Converts who were found guilty of following Jewish practices were frequently tortured and killed.

By the 1470s, the king and queen of Spain, Ferdinand and Isabella, were taking further steps to guarantee Christian purity in their land. First, they required the Jews who had survived to live in their own separate communities. In this way, new Jewish converts to Christianity would be kept away from friends and family members who had remained Jewish and might tempt the converts back to their original faith. Additionally, with the permission of the pope, the king and queen established the Inquisition in Spain. The Inquisition was an organized attempt by the Catholic Church to find, put on trial, and punish any Christian whose loyalty to Christianity seemed questionable. Inquisitors were much-feared investigators and judges whose cruel methods frequently led victims to confess their own supposed heresy or to condemn others. In Spain their major targets were Jews who had recently converted to Christianity.

THE INQUISITION: In the Plaza Mayor of Madrid, accused heretics stand in cages, awaiting their sentencing by judges who sit before them in booths. To the right are effigies and chests of bones to be burnt at the stake in place of heretics who escaped or died before they could be brought to judgment.

Jugement de l'Inquisition dans la grande place de Madrid (Judgment of the Inquisition in the main square of Madrid) by Bernard Picard from Antoine Banier and Jean-Baptiste le Mascrier's *Histoire générale des cérémonies, moeurs, et coutumes religieuses de tous les peuples du monde* (1741). Courtesy of the Pitts Theology Library, Candler School of Theology, Emory University.

HERETICS AT THE STAKE: In the foreground, priests holding crucifixes make a last attempt to encourage the accused heretics to repent, even though it is too late to cancel the punishment. As a sign of shame, the condemned are forced to wear a long, pointed hat and a *sanbenito*, a tunic bearing symbols of the individual's particular sins.

Suplice des condamnez (Punishment of the condemned) by Bernard Picard from Antoine Banier and Jean-Baptiste le Mascrier's *Histoire générale des cérémonies, moeurs, et coutumes religieuses de tous les peuples du monde* (1741). Courtesy of the Pitts Theology Library, Candler School of Theology, Emory University.

The kinds of testimony admitted to Inquisition trials spread panic among recent converts. Because Jewish law prohibits the lighting of fires on the Sabbath, having a chimney that emitted no smoke on a Saturday was considered a powerful indicator that a person was a crypto-Jew. Other indicators included buying lots of vegetables in the springtime or shopping at a butcher shop owned by a recent convert—the first because one might be stocking up for Passover, when it is forbidden to eat bread, and the second because one might be secretly obtaining kosher meat, which comes from certain kinds of animals slaughtered according to a specific set of rules. Once an individual was deemed guilty of being a crypto-Jew, his entire network of family members and friends also fell under suspicion. Convicted heretics were often burnt at the stake.

The physical isolation of the Jews and the ruthless attacks of the Inquisition were apparently insufficient to guarantee the religious purity that Ferdinand and Isabella sought. On March 31, 1492, the royal couple signed an order requiring all remaining Jews to leave the country within just four months. It is difficult for people today to fathom what the royal order must have meant to the horrified Jews who first heard about it. Many of these people had never set foot beyond the few miles surrounding their little communities, and everything beyond was a vast unknown. Their families, their homes, their communities, their synagogues, their livelihoods—their entire world was falling apart, and they knew no other.

It is not surprising that instead of uprooting their entire lives, some Jews decided to remain in Spain by converting to Christianity, despite all the suspicion and potential danger that they would face. But huge numbers of Jews refused to compromise their faith, and after what must have been weeks of grief, despair, and desperate planning, they took whatever belongings they could carry and left. By the end of July 1492, there were officially no Jews remaining in a country that Jews had called home for over a thousand years. Most of the refugees made their way to neighboring Portugal.

Portugal solved the refugees' problem for only a short time. Within four years King Manuel of Portugal, eager to boost his image as a Christian zealot, signed an order forbidding Jews and Muslims from living in his country. Although Muslims faced the terrifying dangers and difficulties of resettlement, they were allowed to leave Portugal with their families intact. Manuel feared that a more aggressive policy would risk reprisals against Christians in Islamic lands. But the situation was different for Jews, who had no powerful advocates anywhere else in the world. Manuel knew that

Jews had brought a lot of money to his country through their active businesses, and he realized that expelling the Jewish population would hurt the country's economy—as had indeed happened in Spain. And so, despite his edict of expulsion, Manuel did not actually give Jews the option of leaving. The Jews in Portugal were given one possibility only: forced conversion to Christianity.

To the recent refugees from Spain, the royal order felt like the return of a nightmare. But soon they discovered that it was not exceptionally difficult to live as crypto-Jews in Portugal. For about fifty years, the forced converts quietly managed to keep their Jewish traditions alive, alive, even after the pope formalized the Portuguese Inquisition in 1536. In 1547, however, the nightmare was back in full force. By that point, administrative disputes that had prevented full implementation of the Inquisition were ironed out, and the Catholic Church began its merciless pursuit of suspected heretics. Portugal's campaign turned out to be so much crueler than the one established by Ferdinand and Isabella that some crypto-Jews chose to return to Spain despite the dangers awaiting them there.

But many of the forced converts decided to sneak their way out of Portugal to try their luck where they would be out of the Inquisition's reach. The families of Michael and Hanna Spinoza were among those

WESTERN EUROPE IN THE SIXTEENTH CENTURY: After
fleeing Portugal, Michael Spinoza and his family probably lived for a
while in the French city of Nantes before they made their way to the
Dutch Republic.

Map based on "Western Europe in the Time of Elizabeth" from
Charles Colbeck, ed. *The Public Schools Historical Atlas*, 2nd ed.
(1885). Butler Library, Columbia University in the City of New York.

who made this bold decision. At some point around 1590, when Michael was a very young boy, his family managed the dangerous escape from Portugal, and by the early 1600s they had settled in Amsterdam. Less is known about Hanna, but she, too, came from a family that had somehow made its way out of Portugal. And now, in 1632, Michael and Hanna were about to circumcise and give a Hebrew name to their newborn son in an ancient Jewish ceremony that they could celebrate openly and fearlessly.

It is certainly tempting to imagine that when Michael and Hanna Spinoza circumcised and named their son, they were thinking about their good fortune to have made it to Amsterdam. In Hebrew, the language of their Jewish tradition, the name they chose was "Baruch," and in Portuguese, the day-to-day language of their community, the name they chose was "Bento." In both languages, the new baby's name meant "blessed."

CHAPTER 2

THE DUTCH
PROMISED LAND

AS BENTO GREW UP, HE WAS CONSTANTLY REMINDED OF just how blessed he was. One of the most powerful reminders came each spring during the holiday of Passover, which celebrates the ancient biblical story of the Hebrew slaves' liberation from their Egyptian oppressors. In Jewish tradition, however, the story has a much larger meaning. Each year at the *seder*, the special evening feast held at the beginning of the holiday, participants read aloud a pronouncement made by the rabbis of long ago: *In every generation, one is obligated to think of oneself as having personally left Egypt.*

Bento must have sat in rapt attention at the *seder*, fighting off sleep as his bedtime came and went. He was a handsome, dark-skinned boy of slight build, quiet and serious. His most prominent feature— large, thoughtful eyes—seemed as deep and dark as wells. Bento would have done his very best to think of himself as one of those freed Hebrew slaves, and it would not have been so difficult after all. In the midst of all the ancient stories, the older members of his extended family would have shared more recent stories of oppression and escape. They had personally left an Egypt of their own.

And there was more. Bento's older relatives had not only left their own Egypt but had made it to their own Promised Land. They had found freedom in the city of Amsterdam, a haven of safety and tolerance so unusual that it staggered the imagination. Bento, of course, already knew the well-worn tales about how Jews had first made their way to Amsterdam. The first Jews had arrived only a few decades earlier, but their stories already had a magical, mythlike quality. One story told about a group of crypto-Jews who had secretly managed to board a ship that was headed from Portugal to the Dutch Republic. The refugees did not know what to expect at their destination, but they knew that the Dutch Republic had recently declared its independence from Spain and that the Republic's largely Protestant population was not especially sympathetic to Catholicism. The Catholic Church would not be setting up an inquisition there. Perhaps, the refugees hoped, the Dutch Republic would allow them to establish a small community and lead quiet, unmolested lives as Jews. At the very least, the place where they were headed could not be any worse than the place that they were leaving.

An unexpected and worrisome turn of events soon put everything at risk. The ship was seized on the high seas by the English and brought to England, a land where Jews had not been allowed to live for hundreds of years. All seemed lost. But the duke who commanded the English ships spotted an exceptionally beautiful woman among the refugees. Her name was Maria Nuñes. The duke fell instantly in love and proposed marriage. The offer was very attractive, but Maria refused it. She had fled Portugal so that she could live openly as a Jew, and she did not intend to lose sight of her goal.

Maria's beauty was so exceptional and the story of the duke's disappointed love so heartbreaking that the English monarch, Queen Elizabeth, took an interest in the situation. Queen Elizabeth arranged to meet with Maria and instantly understood why the duke had fallen in love. The queen herself was so taken by Maria's beauty that she made the young woman her personal companion and introduced her into London's best society. Not wanting to lose her, the queen made her all sorts of generous promises to convince her to stay in England. But the young woman stayed so firm in her determination to reach the Dutch Republic that the queen finally gave in and provided her with the means to achieve her goal. Maria eventually arrived safely in Amsterdam, where she married another Portuguese refugee and established what was—at least according to the story—the first Jewish home in the city. The freedom of Amsterdam was worth more than all the promises of a queen.

Another story told of a different group of Portuguese refugees who secretly boarded two boats headed for Germany. After landing safely in the seaport city of Emden, the refugees wandered through the streets, trying to figure out what to do next. Suddenly they stopped in astonishment at what seemed a miraculous sight: right before them was a home bearing a Hebrew inscription. Few, if any, of the refugees knew how to read Hebrew, as it had been years since they had been able to have any formal Jewish education in Portugal. But they knew enough to recognize Hebrew letters when they saw them.

The home, it turned out, was owned by a Jewish man named Moses Uri Halevi. Moses himself had no language in common with his visitors, but his son Aaron, who knew some Spanish, soon understood that the refugees wanted him and his father to help them start their lives again as Jews. The refugees' very first request was for the Halevis to circumcise the men in their group.

Ever since biblical times, Jewish tradition has understood circumcision as a means of declaring a man's identity as a Jew. But back in Portugal, circumcising a baby boy would have endangered everyone involved. The physical sign of circumcision, unmistakable and permanent, would have provided inquisitors with clear evidence of crypto-Judaism. Crypto-Jews had sorrowfully given up this central Jewish tradition, and over time they had even forgotten how the ritual was to be performed. And now, incredibly, the refugees had found knowledgeable Jews who could help them.

Moses and Aaron Halevi were eager to assist their fellow Jews, but for the time being they had to quiet their visitors' enthusiasm. There was no inquisition in the German town of Emden, but there were other complications. Emden's official religion was Lutheranism, a form of Protestant Christianity, and Jewish traditions could not be performed in the city. But Amsterdam, in the neighboring Dutch Republic, was not bound by such laws. The refugees were to make their way to that city, where they were to rent a specific house. The Halevis would make their way to Amsterdam after they had settled their own affairs in Emden.

Moses and Aaron kept their promise, and in Amsterdam just a few weeks later, the men from Portugal were circumcised in accordance with

Jewish tradition. Soon, under the direction of Moses and Aaron, the refugees quietly began to hold regular prayer services in their rented home. But one Friday night, the neighbors heard the unfamiliar chant of Hebrew prayer and reported the suspicious activity to the authorities. The deputies sent by the sheriff promptly broke into the house, put a quick end to the service, and arrested Moses and Aaron.

The refugees were close to despair at this turn of events. Fortunately, Jacob Tirado, a member of the group, discovered that he could communicate with the authorities in Latin. Tirado explained that the peculiar gathering was a service marking the Jewish Sabbath and that the unfamiliar sounds were prayers chanted in Hebrew. The authorities were relieved—not because they were happy to encounter Jews but because they were more irritated by the prospect of dealing with Catholics. Hostility between Catholics and Protestants had been rocking Europe ever since Martin Luther had launched the Protestant Reformation almost a century earlier. Moses and Aaron Halevi were quickly released. In time, Tirado was able to argue convincingly for official recognition of the Jewish community, including permission to set up a formal congregation for religious services.

Whether or not these stories were completely true, they reflected the refugees' sense of wonder at their newfound safety. The Jews who had escaped the horrors of Spain and Portugal—the Jews who made up Bento's entire world—had found in Amsterdam their Promised Land. Bento would certainly have felt the personal relevance of the words he recited each year at the *seder*: *It is our duty to give every kind of praise and blessing to the One who performed so many miracles for our ancestors and for us. He took us from slavery to freedom, from sadness to happiness, from mourning to celebration, from thick darkness to great light, and from bondage to redemption.* The little boy with the big dark eyes was indeed *Bento* and *Baruch*—truly blessed.

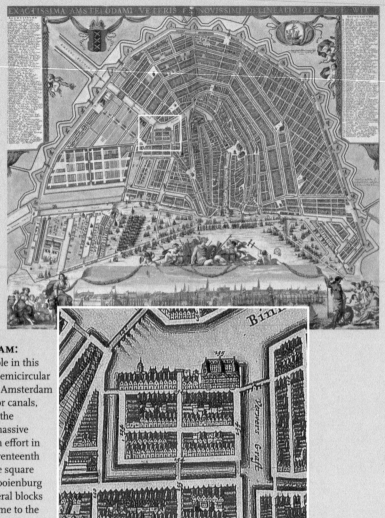

AMSTERDAM:
Clearly visible in this map is the semicircular structure of Amsterdam and its major canals, which were the result of a massive construction effort in the early seventeenth century. The square island of Vlooienburg and the several blocks below it, home to the Jewish community in Spinoza's day, are located just to the left of the city's center.

Map from *Atlas Van der Hagen*, c. 1690, Koninklijke Bibliotheek, The Hague, via https://geheugen.delpher.nl.

CHAPTER THREE

JEWISH LIFE
IN AMSTERDAM

BENTO WAS THE MIDDLE CHILD OF FIVE, RIGHT
between two brother-sister pairs. Miriam and Isaac
were the two oldest, then came Bento, and after him
were Gabriel and Rebecca. The children were quite
close in age to one another. Miriam was only three
years older than Bento, and Isaac was born between
the two of them. The Spinoza home was full of the
busy activities of many young children.

Despite all the blessings for which Bento
and his siblings could be grateful, they endured
more than their share of tragedy. Their mother,
Hanna, was not a healthy woman. She suffered
from chronic lung problems, and she died when
Bento was only six years old. The children's father,
Michael, was left with his hands full. He had to
deal not only with his own loss but also with the
grief and endless needs of so many little children.

In addition, he had a business to maintain. Michael imported various products into the Dutch Republic, especially dried fruit from Spain and Portugal, and he was a reasonably successful merchant who was able to provide his family with a comfortable home. But Michael did not have enough money to neglect his business for long. It must have been a terribly difficult and painful time in the Spinoza household.

The situation improved a few years after Hanna's death. Michael met a woman named Esther Fernand, who had recently arrived from Portugal, and the two were married. Esther raised the children during their formative years, and it is possible that Rebecca, the youngest child, was actually her biological daughter. Since Bento was so young when Hanna died, Esther was the mother he knew best.

During the difficult times they faced, Bento and his family must have found tremendous comfort in their very close-knit community. The Jews of Amsterdam were not forced to live in a ghetto, but most of them did, in fact, choose to live in the same small area. Not surprisingly, the immigrants felt most comfortable living with others who shared their language, their way of life, and their history. In a world of just a few city blocks, the comforting fragrance of traditional Iberian cuisine drifted from windows and doorways, and adults who gathered on street corners spoke animatedly in Portuguese, contrasting, perhaps, the blinding sun of their native land with the cold and damp of their new home. At cultural gatherings, the immigrants reached even further back to the dim memories of Spain from earlier generations. At such events, friends shared the sounds and colors of poems, songs, and stories written in Spanish, the language that the community still associated with literary art and sophistication. Its physical confines may have been small, but Bento's community was part of a grand heritage that spanned many long years and many long miles.

Jewish traditions were also an important part of community life. The weekly Sabbath and the various holidays sprinkled throughout the year meant a steady stream of public worship, celebration, feasting, and social visits. One especially meaningful day was Purim, the joyous carnival holiday that comes at the end of winter. Purim commemorates the events recorded in the biblical Book of Esther, which details the story of long-ago Jews who eluded the Persians who sought to destroy them. The heroine of the story, Queen Esther, was a stunningly beautiful woman who had been brought to the royal palace and married to the Persian king. No one in the palace knew that Esther was really Jewish, a fact she kept hidden even from her royal husband. Esther's concern for her own people, combined with the power she was able to exert in the royal palace, resulted in the dramatic victory of the endangered Jews.

Bento's community identified quite profoundly with Queen Esther. After all, she, too, had been a crypto-Jew—forced to live outwardly like a non-Jew while remaining inwardly loyal to her religion. In fact, many Jews in Amsterdam, given the habits they had inevitably acquired as they posed as Catholics back in Portugal, called the Purim heroine Saint Esther rather than Queen Esther. This was their way of showing how much she meant to them, but the habit irritated the community's rabbis, who kept insisting from the pulpit that Jews do not have saints. Old Catholic habits were sometimes hard for the Jews of Amsterdam to break.

An even deeper appeal of the Purim story was how all its pieces fit together. It did not seem fair that Queen Esther was forced to live as a crypto-Jew, but that was precisely what made it possible for her to save her people. Her personal tragedy turned out to be the path to salvation. Maybe, just maybe, there was a similar sort of purpose behind all the suffering that the crypto-Jews of Spain and Portugal had undergone. God must have had a reason for all that misery.

And that misery was far from over. The Jews of Amsterdam were aware that they were living in a kind of parallel world to the one they had escaped. They could attend synagogue services, circumcise their sons, enjoy their Passover *seders*, celebrate their Purim carnivals, and live other aspects of their Jewish lives in glorious freedom, but back in Spain and Portugal, the Inquisition was in full force. Bento could not have failed to notice the worried whispers of the adults around him. There were still so many people, so many friends and family members, left behind. One of the community's rules absolutely prohibited any mention of Judaism in any letters sent to Spain, because a letter containing such mention could put the life of the recipient at risk. Whenever another precious Jewish soul managed the dangerous escape, it was a reason for the entire community to rejoice. The Jews of Amsterdam were a large, extended family bound together by joy and sorrow. The community had even proudly coined a name for itself: "*la Nação*," Portuguese for "the Nation."

The Nation's neighborhood consisted of two parts, and they were as familiar to Bento as the rooms of his own home. One part was a square island called Vlooienburg, which was bordered on one of its sides by a canal called the Houtgracht. The second part of the neighborhood consisted of a few blocks just across the Houtgracht. It was in that second part, along the canal, that Bento's family lived. The location of Bento's home meant that his family was relatively well off, since in Amsterdam the most desirable and expensive homes were the ones along the canals. Through his front windows, Bento could see the bridge that crossed the Houtgracht and connected the two parts of the Jewish neighborhood. Bento used that bridge several times a day as he went to and from his school, which was located on Vlooienburg, right along the canal.

Bento knew, of course, that anything Jewish in Portugal had been the deepest and darkest of secrets. But for him, open expressions of Judaism were simply a normal way of life. In fact, the main street on his side of the canal, the Breestraat ("Broad Street"), was becoming popularly known as the Jodenbreestraat ("Jews' Broad Street"), and eventually the city made that new name official. His school was not hiding under any disguises, nor were any of the three synagogues that eventually merged into one, moving into a large building located right on the Houtgracht—just eight houses, a warehouse, and an alleyway down from Bento's home. The neighborhood was full of other Jewish establishments as well, and each one clearly proclaimed what it was. There were special butcher shops where Bento's family bought kosher meat. There were stores selling ritual items such as *tallitot*, the striped prayer shawls that men wore in the synagogue, and *mezuzot*, the handwritten

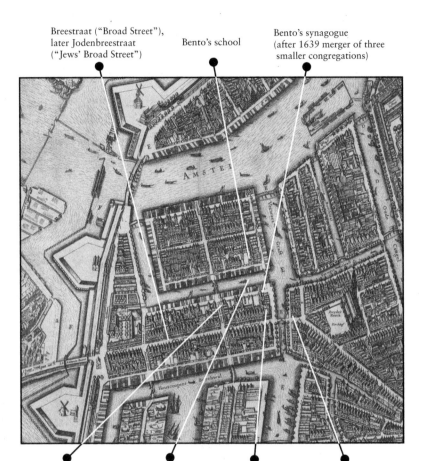

Breestraat ("Broad Street"), later Jodenbreestraat ("Jews' Broad Street")

Bento's school

Bento's synagogue (after 1639 merger of three smaller congregations)

Bento's house

Houtgracht

Rembrandt's house (1639-1658)

Rabbi Mortera's house

MAP OF THE JEWISH NEIGHBORHOOD: As this map suggests, the setting of Bento's daily life was compact and intimate.

Detail from *Plattegrond van Amsterdam (blad middenlinks)* from printmaker Balthasar Florisz. van Berckenrode, 1625. Collection Rijksmuseum, Amsterdam.

parchments in decorative cases that were attached to doorposts. There were bookstores offering prayer books, Bibles, and other Jewish texts. And, of course, there were the people. Portuguese Jews quickly adopted Dutch ways of dressing, imitating the hairstyles, collars, capes, and buckled footwear of the wider world around them. But they remained easily identifiable by their dark skin and dark hair, and the community's several rabbis, with their beards and skullcaps, were unmistakable. Jewish life was so open and so established in Amsterdam that Bento sometimes heard his city called the "Dutch Jerusalem."

Talmud Torah, the Nation's school, was a special source of pride. Bento and his generation would never have to suffer the ignorance of their parents and grandparents, who had been so deprived of Jewish knowledge that they hardly knew how to live as Jews once they arrived in Amsterdam. The Nation was deeply concerned about the Jewish education of its young and was ready to spend the money necessary to make that education possible—at least for boys. Since the home was considered the primary domain of women, it was there that girls were expected to learn everything they needed to know about Jewish life. But for boys, attendance at Talmud Torah was mandatory. The school and its teachers were supported by community funds and private donations, and tuition was free so that even poor children could attend. The curriculum proceeded step by step from the most basic knowledge all the way through advanced rabbinical training for the most gifted students. Within just a couple of decades, the Nation's school system had become the envy of much older and more established Jewish communities elsewhere in Europe.

Children began attending Talmud Torah when they were seven years old. Bento started school shortly after his mother's death, and it must have been comforting to get out of the house and experience the stability of the school day. Each morning Bento crossed the bridge over the Houtgracht and immediately turned right for the short walk to school along the canal. Because the class schedule was divided into two parts, Bento had to make the round trip twice each day. The first block of classes ran for three hours, from 8:00 until 11:00, when the children returned home for lunch. The second part began at 2:00 and generally ended at 5:00. During the midday break, Bento frequently had private tutoring, as did most children from homes that could afford it. When the children were dismissed at the end of the school day, they were expected to attend synagogue for evening prayers before returning home.

Bento was the type of child who loves school—serious, highly intelligent, and excited about learning new things. Since Bento spoke Portuguese with family and friends and Dutch for occasional encounters with non-Jews, it took a while to adjust to Spanish, the language of instruction at Talmud Torah. But Spanish, the language of learning and culture among members of the Nation, was the obvious choice for the classroom. At school he was also learning the even less familiar Hebrew, the language of Jewish tradition. Each part of Bento's life had a language of its own.

In first grade Bento quickly mastered the shapes and sounds of the Hebrew alphabet, and he was soon able to recite aloud the texts that his teacher, the *rubi*, gave him. The texts came from the *siddur*, the traditional prayer book, and during Sabbath services at the synagogue each week, Bento had a welcome chance to show his latest progress to his father.

A total of four grades made up the elementary program, and children usually stayed in each grade for more than a year. Students were promoted only after having mastered the material at their current level, and the process of moving through the four elementary grades usually took about seven years. When Bento proudly moved on to second grade, he entered a classroom full of the earnest, high-pitched voices of boys learning the traditional melody for

THE NATION'S SYNAGOGUE: This converted warehouse on the Houtgracht was originally home to Beth Israel, one of three synagogues serving the Portuguese Jewish community. When the three congregations united in 1639, the building became home to the consolidated synagogue, which took the name Talmud Torah. The school of that name, which Bento attended, was located next door.

The Portuguese Synagogue, Waterlooplein, etching by Romeyn de Hooghe, c. 1686. Stadsarchief Amsterdam.

JEWISH LIFE: Jewish immigrants quickly claimed Amsterdam as their home. In the foreground to the right is the grand Portuguese synagogue established in 1675; to the left are the New Synagogue, built in 1752, and the Great Synagogue, built in 1671, both by Jews from Central and Eastern Europe. Against the buildings' façade, Jews in temporary huts celebrate Sukkot, the Feast of Tabernacles.

View of the Portuguese and High German Synagogues during the Feast of Tabernacles by P. Wagenaar, Jr. (artist) and C. Philips Jacobszoon (engraver) from William Hurd's *Oude En Tegenwoordige Staat En Geschiedenis Van Alle Godsdiensten* (Amsterdam: M. de Bruyn, 1781–1791). Koninklijke Bibliotheek, The Hague, via www.delpher.nl.

public Torah readings. Under the direction of his rubi, he quickly began to sound out the biblical texts and catch on to the melody, and he must have taken great pleasure in his growing ability to sing quietly along with the stately public reading each Sabbath in the synagogue. He would not be able to take official part in those readings until he turned thirteen, the traditional age of Jewish manhood, but he was already well on his way to that next, grand stage of his life.

As a first and second grader, Bento focused on sounding out words and reciting or chanting them aloud. What those words actually meant was the main concern of the third and fourth grades. In third grade, Bento learned to translate the weekly Torah reading from the original Hebrew into Spanish, and in fourth grade, Bento did the same for books of the Bible not included in the public readings. Each child dutifully took his turn reading a verse and then translating it into Spanish. The children were so enthusiastic about this exercise that when the classroom windows were open, a passerby on the street could hear the proceedings quite clearly.

In third and fourth grades, Bento was also introduced to traditional Jewish interpretations of the Torah. According to those interpretations, the Bible is literally the word of God. The text therefore contains nothing accidental and presents the absolute truth about how the world works and is meant to work. But those truths are often conveyed in the barest of hints invisible to the casual or uninformed reader—sometimes just an extra word, an extra letter, or even an extra scribal flourish. Fortunately, the revered rabbis with special access to the text's real meanings handed down a long tradition of written commentaries, enabling any literate Jew to understand the Torah correctly.

The principal commentary in the Talmud Torah curriculum was the work of Rashi, a medieval French Jewish scholar. Bento would certainly have studied Rashi's first question and answer on the Torah. Starting with the assumption that the Torah is a guide to living a Jewish life, Rashi wondered why the text did not simply begin with the first law given to the Jewish people. Why did the text begin instead with the seemingly unnecessary account of God's creation of the world? The answer, according to Rashi, is that the Jewish people might later need the creation account to defend themselves against non-Jews. If the non-Jewish nations of the world ever accused the Jewish people of stealing the land of Israel away from the ancient Canaanites who had once lived there, the Jewish people could respond, "All the earth belongs to the Holy One, blessed be

He; He created it and gave it to whom He pleased. When He willed He gave it to them, and when He willed He took it from them and gave it to us."

Comments like these must have generated within Bento and his classmates a thrilling sense of belonging. By studying the Bible under the guidance of their *rubi*, they were entering a special fellowship that saw beyond everyday surfaces, straight through to God's ultimate purpose for the world. In God's grand blueprint, every single element had its own role to play. And standing right at the center of everything was the Jewish people, the Bible's Chosen People, for whom the entire world had been created.

The sense of entering a special fellowship must have intensified as the boys' thirteenth birthdays neared. Soon each of them would become a *bar mitzvah*, a person obligated to keep all the laws of Judaism. They would be able to participate in the quorum of ten men needed for public prayer, lead synagogue services, and chant from the Torah scroll at public readings. Like all the other men during weekday prayers, they would also don *tefillin*, special leather boxes containing slips of parchment inscribed with biblical passages. Each boy would tie one box onto his forehead and one box onto his arm, indicating that his thoughts as well as his deeds were entirely devoted to God's service.

Bento was a favorite of his teachers. He was not only bright but also respectful, and he made excellent progress throughout his schooling. Michael Spinoza must have treasured every sign of his son's development and taken great pride in his own share in the success. The Jewish education denied to Michael himself could at least be lavished upon his children. Talmud Torah existed because of the hard work of people like Michael, who freely gave his time and energy to committees that established and maintained community institutions. Michael also made generous donations to the Nation's educational system and to other community causes above and beyond the taxes every member of the community was expected to pay.

But Michael, a practical-minded merchant, was aware that living in the world requires more than just the Jewish knowledge that was the entire focus of the Talmud Torah curriculum. Michael was especially concerned to see Bento develop the ability to think critically and to differentiate between truth and falsehood. When Bento was just ten years old, his father put him to the test.

Michael sent Bento to collect some money that was owed by an old woman. When Bento entered the old woman's house, he found her reading her

Bible and praying. She seemed wrapped in her own world as she swayed over the well-worn pages, murmuring in plaintive tones and raising her half-closed eyes toward the ceiling. She did not interrupt herself when she saw the young boy, but motioned for him to wait, and he respectfully stood off to the side in silence. Once she had finished, he explained his errand to her. The old woman counted out the money she owed, placed it on the table, and again began uttering a prayer—this time pronouncing the words clearly enough for Bento to hear. She was asking God to help Bento grow up to be as honest and as good a man as his father. Then she swept up the money and put it into Bento's bag.

But Bento was suspicious. He had been well trained by his father, and even at his young age, he knew that there was a difference between the hollow display of ritual and genuine commitment to piety. Despite the old woman's objections, Bento insisted on counting the money himself, and he quickly discovered that the old woman had indeed tried to cheat him. A closer look at the table revealed a narrow slit through which the woman had obviously dropped some of the coins that she had counted out. Bento demanded the missing coins and was able to bring the entire amount back to his father. Bento had passed his father's test. His keen intelligence, his calm self-confidence, and his ability to assess personalities would certainly serve him well if he chose to follow in his father's line of work. As it turned out, Bento would put those abilities to use in an entirely different way.

CHAPTER FOUR

BEYOND THE JEWISH NEIGHBORHOOD

OF COURSE, THERE WAS A MUCH LARGER WORLD beyond the Nation. Bento had glimpses of it even in the Jewish neighborhood where he spent most of his time, since many non-Jews lived in that area as well. There were the wood dealers who maintained warehouses on Vlooienburg and shipped their merchandise on the Houtgracht, which in fact took its name ("Wood Canal") from their activity. There were numerous artists and art dealers, most notable among them Rembrandt van Rijn, who lived for a while just a few steps from Bento's home and often had Jews from the neighborhood sit as models for his paintings. There were the occasional visits by government officials or by people who had business dealings with merchants like Bento's father. Like other children of the Nation, Bento probably

REMBRANDT: Although this work's earliest title, "Pharisees in the Temple," suggests a biblical setting, Rembrandt probably used contemporary Jewish models for the scene.

Pharisees in the Temple (Jews in the Synagogue) by Rembrandt van Rijn, 1648. Courtesy of the National Gallery of Art, Washington.

Rembrandt may have painted this Jewish doctor, Ephraim Bonus, as payment for medical services. Bonus's attire shows how readily the Portuguese Jews adopted Dutch styles of dress.

Ephraim Bonus by Rembrandt van Rijn, 1647. Courtesy of the National Gallery of Art, Washington.

translated between the Dutch of these visitors and the Portuguese of his home.

And the world beyond the Jewish neighborhood was full of fascinating, ceaseless activity. Bento grew up in the middle of what has become known as the Dutch Golden Age. During this time, the Dutch Republic, the seven northern provinces of the Netherlands, enjoyed a period of astonishing economic growth. Dutch ships traveled the globe in the largest and most complex import-export network the world had yet seen, a network that included Europe, North and South America, Africa, and Asia. To simplify arrangements as well as to thwart the competition of other countries, the Dutch set up trading posts and colonies in strategic locations including Indonesia, Japan, the Caribbean, Brazil, and southern Africa. One such outpost, a small settlement called New Amsterdam, has become especially well known. New Amsterdam was eventually taken over by the English and is now called New York City.

The most important of the seven provinces within the Dutch Republic was Holland, and the most important city in Holland was Amsterdam. During the time that Bento lived there, Amsterdam was unquestionably the beating heart of the Dutch Golden Age. Amsterdam's rapid growth between the late 1500s and mid-1600s is a good measure of just

(TOP) AMSTERDAM'S SHIPS: This image shows men engaged in shipbuilding, a major industry in seventeenth-century Amsterdam. The crush of masts depicted in the background sometimes reminded visitors of trees in a dense forest.

Veue d'Amsterdam (View of Amsterdam), etching by Stefano Della Bella, seventeenth century. Yale University Art Gallery.

(BOTTOM) LABOR AND REST AT THE SHIPYARDS: In this image, the hard labor of the shipbuilders is contrasted by the three men at rest in the rowboat to the left. Two of the men enjoy the relatively new fashion of smoking pipes.

Autre veue d'Amsterdam (Another view of Amsterdam), etching by Stefano Della Bella, seventeenth century. Yale University Art Gallery.

how big a role it played in the country's development. When the seven provinces first joined together in 1579, Amsterdam's population had numbered only about 25,000. But by 1610, the population had already more than doubled and was showing no sign of slowing down. In that year, city planners approved a building project that would quadruple Amsterdam's size as well as turn it into what many residents and visitors considered the most beautiful city in Europe. By 1660, when Bento was in his late twenties, the population had skyrocketed to 200,000.

Walking through the city, Bento could see the many ways in which Dutch people made their money and displayed their wealth. Along the numerous canals and waterways stood the warehouses that temporarily stored goods moving in and out of the city. Workers efficiently loaded and unloaded the ships that sailed all over the world. There were so many ships along the city's waterways that the vast collection of masts, those tall vertical poles that support the sails, sometimes reminded foreign visitors of a massive forest. Even more impressive was that most of these ships were owned by local Amsterdam merchants. By the middle of the 1600s, more merchant ships were owned by residents of Amsterdam than by people in all the rest of Europe combined.

The crates moving on and off those many ships contained items from both near and far: local Dutch products, such as butter, cheese, and herring; goods from other parts of Europe, such as Spanish wool and Swedish metal; and more unusual items from farther afield, such as Indian tea, Japanese silk, or Chinese porcelain. The air was full of the exotic smells of cinnamon, nutmeg, and a strange new drink called coffee. Bento might even have watched the arrival of goods that his father bought and sold as part of his business: dried fruits and citrus from Spain and Portugal, oil from Algeria, and clay pipes for smoking Brazilian tobacco. Pipe smoking was an especially popular activity for both men and women during the Dutch Golden Age.

Not far from the docks were the impressive buildings that housed the two biggest companies involved in international trade, the Dutch East India Company and the Dutch West India Company. As early as 1602, individuals were able to buy shares in the Dutch East India Company and enjoy a portion of the money that the company made—a scheme for investment and profit that resulted in what many historians consider the world's first stock exchange. Nearby was the Bank of Amsterdam, especially helpful to businessmen juggling the monetary systems of various countries. In the same district, insurance companies sold policies to merchants who worried about losing goods at sea.

And then, of course, there were the factories. In Amsterdam's rapidly expanding sugar refineries, the raw material from sugarcane, imported mostly from Brazil, was processed into the familiar white granules. Several of the refineries were owned and run by Portuguese Jews whom Bento recognized from his neighborhood. And over at the shipyards, workers busily constructed the great vessels that would travel to the far reaches of the Earth. At the time, more ships were built in Amsterdam than in any other place in Europe.

Amsterdam's energetic businesses brought the people of the city a great deal of money. A walk along the city's canals would have taken Bento past the enormous mansions and spacious townhouses of the most successful merchants. Amsterdam's less prosperous population clustered in the crowded interior of the city's many islands, but even in those darker backstreets, most people enjoyed a much higher standard of living than they would have had in other parts of the world.

Amsterdam's residents were famously concerned about cleanliness, and at any given time, numerous housekeepers were energetically sweeping and scrubbing the front stoops of their homes. If Bento had managed to look past the housekeepers and through the front doors of the finest homes, he might have glimpsed some of the exotic luxuries brought by Amsterdam's many ships from far and wide—gorgeously carved furniture decorated with panels of ebony or ivory, expensive velvets and silks dyed in the richest of colors, Turkish rugs woven in complicated patterns, Chinese porcelain bowls holding a selection of mouthwatering foods. People who could not afford these luxuries found ways to imitate the people who could. The Dutch city of Delft, for instance, produced blue-and-white pottery that was a reasonable stand-in for Chinese porcelain, and Flanders, just to the south of the Dutch Republic, offered local woolen rugs in popular Turkish patterns.

And everywhere there were paintings, even in the homes that did not seem especially grand. Oil paintings were all the rage in the Dutch Republic, and the prices that they fetched were within the range of people with average incomes. Many canvases celebrated the plenty that people enjoyed: heaps of good food, festive celebrations, and elegantly dressed families in their beautifully furnished homes.

The eagerness to buy and enjoy luxury items was especially evident in the first few years of Bento's lifetime during a bizarre episode that has come to be known as "tulip mania." Tulips had only recently made their way from Turkey to Holland, where their exotic beauty turned them into highly desired symbols of wealth and status. Before long, large numbers of people began spending absurd amounts of money to acquire the rarest varieties of the flower. At the height of the craze, a single bulb of a particularly coveted variety fetched a staggering price that equaled approximately four tons of wheat, four tons of rye, four fat oxen, eight pigs, a dozen sheep, over one hundred gallons of wine, four tons of butter, a thousand pounds of cheese, a bed, some clothing, and a silver pitcher.

But it was never just a single buyer purchasing a bulb from a single seller. Along the way to the final sale was a long chain of transactions. Each buyer in the chain hoped to make a profit by selling his purchase as quickly as possible to another buyer willing to pay just a bit more. The pace grew so rapid that soon the bulbs themselves were not being transferred hand to hand. In fact, soon the bulbs did not even exist when the transactions were being made. What was being bought and sold was nothing more than a paper promise for the future delivery of bulbs as yet to be produced—a promise that in today's financial language would be called a "future." As tulip season approached, excitement about the flowers grew, and there were always buyers ready to pay more for futures.

odiga rerum Luxuries, nunquam parvo contenta paratu. Lucan. 4. lib.
2 fc. et exi. Amstelad. *cum Privil. ord. Holland.*

MATERIAL PLENTY:
This typical still life celebrates luxury at the same time that it advocates simplicity. The Latin quotation at the bottom, from the Roman poet Lucan, reads, "Oh, lavish luxury, never contented with the frugal meal!"

Still Life with a Hanging Partridge by Pieter Schenck I, late seventeenth century. Courtesy of the National Gallery of Art, Washington.

There was, of course, a natural limit to the buying and selling. At a certain point, the actual tulip bulbs would be delivered to the last buyer in the chain, the one who had paid the highest price for the futures but had not managed to sell them in time to someone else. That final person would not make any money at all but would be stuck paying an outrageous amount of money for a handful of onion look-alikes that held the promise of a few pretty flowers. As one historian describes it, tulip mania was really a game of hot potato. The idea was to pass along the futures as quickly as possible and not be stuck with them when the high-risk game ended.

The game ended badly. In 1637, when Bento was four years old, the leadership of Holland decided that the craze had become too dangerous, with too many people thoughtlessly risking everything they owned. The government's solution was simply to put an immediate stop to the whole affair. Panic swept through the city as people who still held futures tried desperately to sell them off. Tulip prices dropped quickly and steeply, and investors who had hoped for a huge profit ended up losing everything instead. Sanity had been restored, but many individuals were plagued for years, often for the rest of their lives, by the debts they still owed.

Tulip mania was certainly an unusual episode, but its basic outline fit the spirit of the times:

the zestful pursuit of wealth and the hearty enjoyment of all that money could buy. If spending money to buy all sorts of luxuries is what brings people happiness, then the merchant families of Amsterdam were happy indeed.

Of course, Amsterdam, like any other city, had its more unfortunate side. Not everyone could afford the pleasures that the merchants enjoyed, and the more severely underprivileged often resorted to begging or crime. To alleviate the problem, the city distributed money to the poor on a weekly basis, and many of the wealthiest merchants funded orphanages, hospitals, and community homes for the needy. These efforts were motivated by fear as much as by generosity, since it would take very little for the underprivileged to unite against the prosperous classes. This fear tugged constantly at the wealthy and powerful, and it helps to explain the city's inhumanity toward the poor who turned to crime. Captured criminals were branded with hot irons, tortured, or executed. Gallows, deemed more effective than the city's several prisons—and certainly much less expensive—were conveniently positioned at each of the city's gates. The city's approach to crime was relatively successful. The poor did not often disturb the general peace.

Bento had little contact with the darker side of the city. For the most part, the Nation's many

TAB. CCLXI.
(a)

Tulipa Persica

Tulipa flore vario
alias Lilio
narcissus.

(LEFT) TULIPS: This illustration, from one of the lavish botanical catalogues that were popular in the seventeenth century, shows Europe's growing fascination with the exotic Turkish flower.

Illustration of tulips by Jan Theodor de Bry from *Florilegium novum, hoc est Variorum Maximeque Radiorum Florum ac Plantorum*, c. 1612–1618. Yale University Art Gallery.

(ABOVE) TULIP MANIA: Enthroned on a wagon, Flora, the goddess of flowers, holds bunches of tulips as members of her entourage drink, exhibit bags full of money, and entice a crowd of men and women to abandon their honest work. A monkey on the mast discharges excrement on the revelers as a woman releases a bird to signify the loss of hope and innocence. Up ahead, a similar wagon is already floundering at sea.

Flora's Mallewagen, attributed to printmaker Crispijn van de Passe (II), 1637. Collection Rijksmuseum, Amsterdam.

merchants, including Bento's own father, were avid participants in Amsterdam's astounding growth and prosperity. The Portuguese Jews had a peculiar commercial advantage. Their friends and family members, fleeing the Inquisition, had scattered all over the world, creating a large network of people especially inclined to help one another. Aside from providing instant contacts for international trade, this network helped the Jews of Amsterdam overcome specific obstacles that hindered their Christian neighbors. The Dutch Republic was still in the thick of an eighty-year-long struggle to free itself from Spanish rule, and for most of the war's duration, Spanish rulers prohibited any direct trade between Spain and the Dutch Republic. To make matters worse, the prohibition included Portugal, with which the Spanish rulers had close ties, as well as Spanish and Portuguese colonies in the rest of the world. As a result, the average Dutch merchant was cut off from many of the most lucrative trading routes and most highly desired products. But the Portuguese Jews of Amsterdam could tap into the international network of Jewish refugees to work around the prohibition. By sending or receiving goods through family members or old friends who now lived in neutral countries like France, the merchants of the Nation were sometimes able to hide the Dutch origins of their trade.

As Bento dreamed about his future, he might well have imagined himself working by his father's side in the world's greatest city. Bento's older brother Isaac had already joined their father's firm and begun his own career as a merchant. At other times, Bento might have imagined a different life altogether, a quieter one rooted more firmly within the Jewish community. Most students left Talmud Torah after completing the four elementary grades, but there were also fifth and sixth grades, which together lasted an additional six years or so. Those two grades were the crown jewels of the Nation's educational system, and the community set aside special funds to support the students who enrolled. It was in those grades that promising young men engaged in the advanced studies necessary to become rabbis.

Bento must have loved his glimpses of the expansive world beyond his neighborhood, but by nature he was the quiet, thinking sort who enjoyed books and solitude, and his Jewish studies had captured both his heart and his mind. In the meantime, Bento was still in the elementary grades, young enough for his options to remain open, enticing, and perhaps a bit daunting.

DUTCH MUSKETEER: A soldier balances his musket on a support as he blows on his match—one of forty-three movements that musketeers must master, according to the influential military manual *Wapenhandelinghe van roers musquetten ende spiessen*. First published in 1607, the manual was developed by Dutch leaders responsible for conducting the war of independence against Spain.

A Soldier on Guard Blowing the Match by Jacques de Gheyn II, c. 1597. Image courtesy of the Getty's Open Content Program, Getty Research Institute.

CHAPTER FIVE

QUESTIONS AND POTENTIAL CONSEQUENCES

BENTO WAS ABOUT FIFTEEN YEARS OLD WHEN HE began to question the familiar certainties of his life. He felt the change most keenly at school, but no one could tell that anything was happening behind those large dark eyes. Bento remained as serious and thoughtful as ever. He obediently took his turn at reading and translating and seemed engaged enough in learning the traditional biblical commentaries. He was the excellent student he had always been.

But the things that Bento was learning were beginning to feel hollow. Bento had many, many questions. If Moses is really the author of the first five books of the Torah, as Bento's teachers claimed, then how is it possible for those books to contain information that Moses could not possibly have known, such as the circumstances of his own death and its effects on the people he was leading? If experience shows that nature always follows set patterns—that spring will always follow winter, for instance—then isn't it possible that the Torah calls a particular event a miracle simply because ancient people did not grasp the natural pattern behind the event? If the world is full of many different kinds of people, Jews as well as non-Jews, how can it possibly make sense to call one group "chosen" and to dismiss everyone else as second-rate? Bento's list of questions went on and on, and it kept growing. Perhaps the most gnawing, basic question was this one: if the things one is meant to believe don't stand up to logical thinking, where does one find the truth?

Amidst the usual reciting, translating, memorizing, and repeating that were the main activities of the school day, Bento finally got up the nerve to ask some of his questions. Like the other children of the Nation, he had been trained to have a high regard for the religious leaders of his community, and he eagerly looked to his *rubi* for guidance. The *rubi* had devoted many years to studying the Torah and the commentaries of the great rabbis. He must certainly have wondered about some of these troubling questions himself, and he must just as certainly have come up with carefully considered answers.

Bento's expectations were quickly dashed. His *rubi* had nearly the same answer for every question: "That's the way God willed it" or "That's what we believe." His teacher might insist, for instance, that Moses did in fact write about his own death and that he was able to do so because God had given him prophetic knowledge of what would occur. Considering the question answered, the *rubi* would begin moving on to the next topic. But Bento would ask for permission to speak again, and he would respectfully point out that such a notion was not supported by the text itself, which is narrated not by Moses himself but by someone talking *about* Moses. One could arrive at the *rubi*'s conclusion, in other words, only by twisting the text's plain and obvious meaning. At this point Bento would be so eager to support his point that he would fail to notice the increasing dismay on his teacher's face. Bento would rush headlong into a list of other biblical passages he had been compiling, passages referring to geographical names or historical events that dated from long after Moses's time. Those passages, too, suggested that the Torah was written by someone other than Moses.

At this point Bento would be forced to recognize his *rubi*'s dismay—or was it anger? The *rubi* would cut off the discussion before Bento could even finish presenting the first item on his list. "The whole Torah was given us through Moses our Teacher entirely from God," the *rubi* would intone, quoting from one of the well-worn books on his table. "[I]t came to us through Moses who acted like a secretary taking dictation."

The ground was shifting beneath Bento's feet. The exciting, secret meanings that had once thrilled him were growing less and less convincing. Those meanings were beginning to feel more and more like fantasies, like wild perversions of the simple truth. But what shocked Bento most about his *rubi*'s answers was the lack of curiosity they betrayed. Claiming that something is the will of God or that something is an article of faith did not seem to Bento like much of an answer at all; it began to seem like just a silly way to say, "I don't know." Even worse, it meant a refusal to consider the evidence and a willingness to remain in ignorance. And every so often another very critical thought would cross Bento's mind. If a religious leader claimed that something was an article of faith, then anyone who questioned it was in violation of that faith. In effect, there was no way to argue without being labeled a sinner. How terribly easy it was for a religious leader to control an individual or even a whole community.

These were certainly not reactions that Bento expressed aloud. At this point, such thoughts were faint but disquieting ideas that he needed to consider more fully. Furthermore, he was not a troublemaker, and he had no desire to annoy, embarrass, or offend others. So Bento pretended to be satisfied with the answers he had received. He wrote those answers down, contenting himself with his plan to return to them later and give them more thought. And he simply stopped asking any more questions. The *rubi* probably reacted with relief, thinking that his student's unpleasant questions and doubts had finally resolved themselves. Bento's doubts, however, continued to grow, and the questions that he kept to himself became more and more insistent.

As the months passed, Bento could not have failed to recognize that he had embarked on a dangerous path. It was not just a question of angering his teacher. His community had no tolerance for ideas that challenged traditional ways of thinking. Just a few years earlier, a huge scandal had erupted over a man who had publicly questioned the authority of the rabbis and the immortality of the soul. Bento had been only about eight years old when the whole thing hurtled to its end, but that end was too terrifying to be forgotten.

CHAPTER FIVE: QUESTIONS AND POTENTIAL CONSEQUENCES

The man at the center of the scandal was Uriel da Costa, who had lived as a crypto-Jew in Portugal before making his way to Amsterdam to live an openly Jewish life. Since da Costa had never been part of a formal Jewish community in his native country, the Judaism that he knew was based entirely on his own reading of the Bible. Once in Amsterdam, da Costa was shocked by what he found. The Judaism of the Nation certainly had its core in the Bible, but it also included a large number of additions and changes that had been made by the rabbis over many centuries and that had long become mainstream parts of the religion. One such development was the idea that the soul never dies but lives on after the death of the body. Da Costa had seen no evidence for that idea in the Torah itself and was convinced that it was not genuinely part of Judaism.

Da Costa wanted to share the truth with others and soon wrote a book asserting that the Bible is the only source of religious authority in Judaism. He roundly criticized the rabbis for having contaminated Judaism with foreign beliefs and with endless, meaningless rules. The Nation's response was to declare a *cherem* against da Costa.

Cherem (with the *ch* pronounced in a guttural way, like the *j* in Spanish) is a Hebrew word meaning "excommunication," the limiting or suspending of

66

a person's membership in a religious community. The Nation used *cherem* in the same way that a school might use suspension—as a temporary punishment intended to emphasize the seriousness of a wrongdoing. *Cherem* was an attempt to make the sinner feel so unpleasantly isolated that he or she would do whatever was required to rejoin the community.

Cherem varied in length as well as in other specifics. During the period of punishment, which might last a day, a week, a month, or even longer, other members of the community were not allowed to have any contact with the excommunicated person. This restriction might include even family members, and the social isolation could be devastating. Given the close business contacts among members of the Nation, this isolation could also mean a serious loss of income. Additionally, excommunicated individuals were restricted in their ability to participate in religious events. An individual might be excluded from specific prayers or activities in the synagogue or forbidden from entering the synagogue entirely. Relatives of the excommunicated individual might also be denied participation in life-cycle ceremonies. A newborn son might not be circumcised, an eligible daughter might not be married, and a deceased parent might not receive a proper funeral.

A formal ceremony emphasized the seriousness of the crime and its punishment. The community gathered in the synagogue, where the declaration of the *cherem* was read aloud by the rabbi, usually in the presence of the person about to be excommunicated. The declaration presented a history of the sinner's crime as well as the details of the punishment. The gloomy reading was accompanied by blasts of a *shofar*, a ram's horn associated in Jewish tradition with God's judgment. Members of the community sometimes held candles made of black wax, which were pointedly extinguished after the declaration of *cherem* was read. In some ceremonies, the candles were held upside down so that the melting wax would drip into a container filled with animal blood. The ceremony was meant to be frightening, and it must have made a lasting impression on the excommunicated individual as well as on the other participants.

Da Costa's initial response to his *cherem* was hostile. He proceeded to publish a second book that supplemented his anti-rabbinical attacks with his arguments against the soul's immortality. After a while, however, the *cherem* worked as intended. Da Costa could no longer tolerate his social isolation and decided to rejoin the Jewish community. But his return to the fold was only halfhearted. He ridiculed his own attempts to adhere to Jewish practices as "aping the apes," and he was soon caught eating non-kosher food and making negative comments about Judaism to Christians. This time around, the Nation issued a stronger *cherem*, the toughest one that the Amsterdam community had ever imposed. But even with this second *cherem* da Costa was offered another chance. By confessing his sins and allowing himself to be whipped, he would be forgiven and readmitted to the community.

Da Costa managed on his own for seven long years during his second *cherem*, but by the end of that period he had grown so poor and lonely that he finally gave in. Men and women filled the synagogue, watching as da Costa climbed the *bima* at the center of the sanctuary to read his confession aloud. This confession had been composed not by da Costa himself but by the leaders of the Nation, who forced da Costa to say that he deserved to die a thousand times over for his sins and to promise that he would never return to his evil ways. After his mechanical recitation of the required words, da Costa stepped down from the *bima*. As instructed, he undressed down to the waist and removed his shoes. The presiding officials then tied his hands around a pillar and lashed him thirty-nine times, his tortured cries and moans filling the hall with each crack of the whip. When da Costa's hands were untied, he collapsed onto the floor.

Da Costa was pronounced free of the *cherem*, but he had not yet come to the end of his public humiliation. After getting dressed again, he was forced to lie across the threshold of the synagogue so the people of the congregation could step over him as they left the building. But even this final, terrible scene was not the end of the horror. Da Costa went home, where he recorded his fury and shame in an autobiography that he wrote over the course of a few days. He accused the Nation of behavior unworthy even of monkeys. When da Costa was finished writing, he killed himself.

Most people in the Nation dismissed da Costa as a crazy, unbalanced man with absurd ideas. He was a misfit, sadly unable or perversely unwilling to recognize the beauty of authentic Judaism, the Judaism that the Nation so lovingly tended and lived. But some of da Costa's ideas were starting to make a lot of sense to Bento.

CHAPTER SIX

DOUBTING
THE IMMORTALITY
OF THE SOUL

BENTO WAS ALREADY WELL ON HIS WAY TO DA COSTA'S rejection of the soul's immortality. The Torah never explicitly says that the soul continues to exist after death, and in the biblical context, even the different Hebrew words usually translated as "soul" appear to refer simply to the breathing or the life force that leaves us when we die. Given the lack of biblical evidence—not to mention the lack of evidence from our own experience—why did Jewish thinkers constantly claim that the soul outlasts the body? It was obviously best for Bento to keep his doubts on the matter to himself. Da Costa's experience suggested that the immortality of the soul was an especially touchy subject for the Nation.

Judaism traditionally views God as a judge who rewards good people and punishes bad people. Everyday experience, however, shows that good people often suffer and bad people often live quite comfortably. As a judge, then, God seems either incapable or unfair. But such conclusions are completely insupportable to Judaism, which views God as a perfect judge, absolutely good, all-knowing, and all-powerful.

The notion of an afterlife readily resolves this conflict between everyday experience and belief in God's perfect judgment. With an afterlife, the score does not need to be settled while people are still alive in this world. If good people suffer or bad people enjoy themselves, we can rest assured that they will all receive exactly what they deserve after their deaths. Of course, for the idea of an afterlife to make any sense, something has to remain of a person after he or she dies, and that something is the soul.

The immortality of the soul was an emotionally charged topic for the Portuguese Jews of Amsterdam because of their troubled history. When they had lived under the shadow of the Inquisition, they had been forced to violate the demands of their own religion and participate in Catholic rites that, in their eyes, were a form of idolatry, one of the gravest sins imaginable. Fortunately, they had made it to Amsterdam, where they had managed to reform

THE JEWISH CEMETERY: Establishing a Jewish cemetery was one of the earliest concerns of the Spanish and Portuguese Jews who settled in Amsterdam. In 1614 the tiny community acquired land in the village of Ouderkerk, a short distance from Amsterdam along the Amstel River. Most members of the Nation, including Spinoza's parents, were buried there.

Begraef-plaets der Joden, buyten Amsteldam (Jewish Cemetery outside Amsterdam) etching by Abraham Blooteling, after Jacob van Ruisdael, 1670. Courtesy of the National Gallery of Art, Washington.

their ways and reclaim their Judaism. But friends and relatives who had not escaped were still living under the Inquisition. Those ill-fated individuals might be doomed to live their entire lives in sin.

Tormented by the fate of those left behind, the Nation clung desperately to the notion of an afterlife in which all would be set right. God, with infinite compassion, would overlook sins committed under tragic circumstances and would lovingly welcome the sinners' souls into heaven. True, a period of cleansing punishment might be necessary first, but ultimately the souls of the unfortunate sinners would find their well-deserved happiness and tranquility.

The need for this belief was so profound that when a major rabbi in Amsterdam, Rabbi Saul Mortera, began suggesting otherwise, the community suffered a rift that almost tore it apart. The controversy had raged when Bento was just a toddler. Rabbi Mortera—who was originally from Venice and did not share the troubled past of the Nation—argued that Jews who violate the most fundamental aspects of Judaism are forever denied happiness in the afterlife. Because Jews living under the Inquisition were in fact committing those sorts of major violations every day of their lives, their souls would be punished accordingly. For Mortera, the issue was black and white: under all circumstances, Jews were required to choose death over violation of Jewish law.

A public outcry greeted Mortera and his harsh position. Many Portuguese Jews in Amsterdam already had an uneasy relationship with Mortera, who often grew impatient or frustrated with community members who were not entirely faithful to the mainstream Judaism that he was trying to teach them. But Mortera was undeniably a great scholar—arguably the most learned rabbi in the community—and his position was supported by the influential Jewish community of Venice, to which the Nation often looked for religious guidance. The controversy eventually subsided, but it left many scars.

Despite the deep disagreement between the two sides in the dispute, there was one major shared assumption—that the soul is immortal. For both sides, the idea of the soul's immortality helped everything make sense. In Rabbi Mortera's harsh view, sinners who failed to sacrifice their lives to avoid sin would find their comeuppance in the future, even if their lives seemed pleasant enough in the present. In the community's generous view, sinners forced into sin by terrible circumstances beyond their control would be vindicated by a compassionate God who understood the entire situation. The Jews of Amsterdam held fast to

REWARD AND PUNISHMENT: This illustration uses traditional Christian imagery to depict judgment after death. The archangel Michael holds a set of scales; on one side appears a naked baby, representing a dead person's soul, and on the other side appears a collection of fiendish creatures, representing the devil or sin. Fortunately for the soul in this woodcut, the scale tips in the direction of salvation.

The Archangel Michael Weighing a Soul by Lucas Cranach the Elder, 1506. Courtesy of the National Gallery of Art, Washington.

the comforting notion that the world, despite its sometimes chaotic appearance, is part of a neat and orderly system governed by God. Belief in the soul's immortality was vital to that notion.

There was an additional reason for a steadfast belief in the soul's immortality. Most members of the Nation viewed a divine system of reward and punishment, including heaven and hell in the afterlife, as the essential foundation of morality. Individuals are good not because they see goodness as an end in itself but only because they expect prizes for appropriate behavior and penalties for inappropriate behavior. This is like saying that students will work hard only if their parents promise a reward for good grades or a punishment for bad grades. Completely absent is the notion of students who might work hard because they find genuine pleasure and value in their studies and who would feel a loss if they did not apply themselves. In such a view of morality, once the promise of reward or the threat of punishment vanishes, there is simply no reason for good behavior. Evil will rapidly become the norm, and all of society will fall apart.

In short, the Nation had to assume the soul's immortality in order to maintain two fundamental parts of its worldview: belief in a divine plan and morality based on rewards and punishments.

Questioning the immortality of the soul meant attacking the very core of Jewish belief.

It was not just Jewish belief that was concerned. When da Costa attacked the rabbis' authority to make additions and changes to biblical Judaism, the controversy was mostly contained within the Jewish community. But as soon as da Costa wrote his second book, the one that presented his arguments against the soul's immortality, it was not just the Nation that took offense. At that point, even Christians were outraged, and they were outraged for the same reasons as the Jews. Like Judaism, Christianity views God as presiding over an intelligent plan for the universe, and this plan includes a final reckoning in the afterlife. And, like Jews, most Christians of the time viewed reward and punishment as the basis for moral behavior. Da Costa's denial of the soul's immortality was just as profound an attack on Christianity as it was on Judaism.

When Amsterdam's authorities heard about da Costa's second book, they took immediate action to protect the good people of the city against his harmful influence. City officials jailed da Costa for ten days, required him to pay a fine, and burned his book, of which only one copy is known to survive today. Even the fabled tolerance of Amsterdam had its limits.

Thinking can be a dangerous activity—
and it was particularly so in Europe during the
seventeenth century. But ideas do not stop emerging
simply because others disapprove of them. Bento
could not prevent himself from doubting the
immortality of the soul, and his doubts led him to
even more treacherous territory. If people felt less
insecure and adrift in the world, would they need to
look to an afterlife in which all the scores are settled?
If people recognized that good behavior is its own
reward and bad behavior is its own punishment,
would they need to believe in a heaven or a hell?
To what degree are religious beliefs and behaviors
shaped by people's needs and desires?

It was only a very short step from those questions
to a pointed realization: the need or desire to believe
in an idea does not make that idea true.

CHAPTER SEVEN

THE MANY FORCES OF INTOLERANCE

IF BENTO HAD WANTED TO LOCATE AMSTERDAM'S most extreme forces of intolerance, a short walk from his home would have taken him to the Zuiderkerk, the Southern Church. This church, part of the city's massive urban planning and construction in the early 1600s, had recently joined the much older Oude Kerk (Old Church) and Nieuwe Kerk (New Church), which stood in the ancient city center. There were two other churches of recent vintage, the Noorderkerk (Northern Church) and the Westerkerk (Western Church), and plans were afoot for the Oosterkerk (Eastern Church). The placement of the new churches in the four cardinal directions of the city was not only aesthetic but symbolic: God is everywhere, and one's obligation to God exists wherever one goes.

Those imposing houses of worship were all part of the Dutch Reformed Church, the largest and most privileged religious group in the Dutch Republic. The Dutch Reformed Church was based on Calvinism, a particularly strict form of Protestantism. Calvinism stressed the awesome, unfathomable power of God and demanded simple and sober living in absolute obedience to the church. Among their other convictions, Calvinists in Bento's day believed that the church needed to be involved in the kinds of tasks that are usually handled by the government, such as the lawful behavior of citizens, the education of children, the monitoring of business, and the holding of public office. Because religion was meant to touch every aspect of a person's life, the separation of church and state was unthinkable.

At the time, Calvinists throughout Europe often looked to the Swiss city of Geneva as the ideal Christian community and the best model of partnership between church and state. John Calvin, the founder of the movement, was Geneva's spiritual leader for many years, and he helped expand the church's role far beyond providing religious services. In Geneva, the church was responsible for social programs such as aiding the poor, caring for orphans and widows, and running the city hospital. Even sanitation, including an innovative sewage system, fell under the church's supervision. A committee of church elders kept watch over every individual's life and ensured that all residents were living according to the strict rules of Calvinism.

Religious diversity was not to be tolerated in such a place, and, not surprisingly, Geneva had quite a dark side. The committee of church elders overseeing the city's religious life relied on a fearsome network of spies to pry mercilessly into the private lives of citizens. Punishable crimes included cursing, dancing, playing cards, wearing fancy clothes, getting drunk, and laughing in church. For these relatively minor violations, offenders might be whipped or have their tongues pierced. In the most severe cases of disobedience or outspoken rejection of church doctrine, the sinner would be forced out of the city or put to death.

The *predikanten*, the ministers of the Dutch Reformed Church, might have been quite happy to put such practices into place in their own communities. The *predikanten* were deeply troubled by the Dutch Republic's seemingly limitless focus on accumulating wealth and enjoying what money could buy. Such a focus on the things of this world, they felt, was a kind of drunkenness that led people away from the simple piety and devotion to God that comprise the true life of a Christian. Wasn't tulip mania proof that something was rotten at the core of Dutch life? Another thorn in the side of the *predikanten* was Amsterdam's increasingly diverse population. Anyone with a different view of the truth compromised the uniform, God-fearing society that the Calvinists hoped to establish.

Fortunately, at least for minorities like the Jews, the strict Calvinist leaders did not have the upper hand in determining public policy. Local, provincial, and national governments in the Dutch Republic were oligarchies—small, privileged, and insular assemblies of especially powerful people. These people were almost always the country's most prominent merchants, and their priorities often clashed with those of the *predikanten*. Amsterdam's merchant oligarchy was far more concerned about the city's economic well-being than about matters of religious doctrine, and although they considered themselves Christians, they were willing to compromise on religious purity when it made good commercial sense to do so. These political leaders recognized that the city's generally tolerant environment was contributing to its international preeminence as a center of trade. They knew, for instance, that the ambitious and energetic Portuguese Jewish merchants who had recently settled in their midst were bringing good money and good business to Amsterdam.

So while the strict Calvinists of the Dutch
Reformed Church pulled in one direction, the
more liberal merchant oligarchy pulled in the other
direction. Throughout Bento's life, these two forces
jockeyed for control of Amsterdam and the Dutch
Republic. This tension meant that the position of the
Nation was never entirely guaranteed. As long as the
merchants were in charge, the Jewish population
was relatively secure, but the balance could shift at
any moment.

What made matters even more complicated for
the Nation was that the tolerance of the merchant
oligarchy had its limits, too. Da Costa had been
jailed and fined not by the strict Calvinists but by the
supposedly more open-minded political authorities.
In fact, Dutch officials had never been especially
enthusiastic about the Jews in their midst. In 1616,
when the Jewish population had first grown large
enough to concern the politicians in charge of
Holland, the province in which Amsterdam was
located, a special committee was set up to advise
the government on the situation. One of the most
respected members of that committee, Hugo
Grotius, described his regret that Jews had been
allowed to settle in the country at all. Accepting
the Jews, said Grotius, had been a bad decision
based on an improper desire for the wealth that the
newcomers could bring. But what was done was

done. Given that the Jews had already been admitted to the country, Grotius concluded, "Plainly, God desires them to live somewhere. Why then not here rather than elsewhere?" This was hardly a loving embrace of welcome, and it was accompanied by specific measures to limit the supposed damage that Jews could wreak on their Christian neighbors. To ensure an unbridgeable divide between Jews and Christians, the government demanded that Jews live strictly according to the rules of their own religion.

With the horrors of the Inquisition in recent memory, Jewish leaders took with utmost seriousness their obligation to keep their Dutch hosts happy. Community officials made every effort to ensure that no member of the Nation offended Dutch authorities in any way, whether through noisy holiday celebrations, unpleasant begging on the streets, inappropriate discussions with non-Jews, or public expression of unpopular views. And, of course, every Jew was expected to remain loyal to the beliefs and practices of Judaism—not only because of an inward concern about the Nation's spiritual health but also because of an outward worry about the Nation's standing with its Dutch hosts. A Jew who departed in any way from Judaism was not just an individual soul gone astray from the truth but a menace to the safety of the entire Nation.

And so there were countless numbers of enemies
to be made by a Jew who thought and expressed
unpopular ideas. There were religious purists within
the Nation, people like Rabbi Mortera, who would
not tolerate deviations from the Jewish tradition
that they viewed as the indisputable truth. There
were leaders of the Nation who might have been
more flexible in their own responses to the Jewish
tradition but were constantly afraid of offending
their Dutch hosts. There were the *predikanten* of
the Dutch Reformed Church, who saw the Jewish
community as an obstacle to religious uniformity
and a spur to the city's unseemly obsession with
money-making. And there were the members of
the merchant oligarchy who walked a fine line
amidst conflicting concerns: the realization that
diversity and tolerance had contributed significantly
to Amsterdam's economic success, the awareness
that they could maintain their own power only by
keeping the city's Calvinists happy, and the fear that
social disorder would result from views even they
found unacceptable. Even in the most open-minded
city in Europe, forces of intolerance smoldered and
threatened to erupt unexpectedly.

CHAPTER EIGHT

THE FRUSTRATED
MERCHANT

ALTHOUGH BENTO OFTEN FOUND HIS CLASSES AT
Talmud Torah unsatisfactory, being at school at
least gave him time to think through some of the
ideas whirling around in his head. But when Bento
was just seventeen, tragedy struck. Isaac, Bento's
older brother, died. Isaac had been working with
their father, and now Michael Spinoza needed an
extra pair of hands. If Bento had still been thinking
about rabbinical training, it was now a moot point.
Bento left school to become a merchant like his
father.

This was a difficult time in Bento's life. Two
years after Isaac's death, Bento's older sister Miriam
died, leaving behind her husband and their infant
son. Two years later, Bento's stepmother died, and
just five months after that, Michael was dead. In the
space of five years, Bento had lost his older brother,

his older sister, the only mother he had ever really known, and his father. The shock and grief would have been overwhelming enough, but there was also the problem of money. Michael had left behind various debts and financial commitments, and the family business was going through a tough time. At the age of twenty-one, Bento was the senior member of the family. He was in charge, whether he liked it or not.

Bento took on his younger brother, Gabriel, as his business partner, and together they managed to keep the business afloat. At the very beginning, Bento might have appreciated the new scenes, the new faces, and the new challenges, and also have enjoyed the exhilarating allure of profit and public recognition. But any excitement he felt was soon replaced by a burdensome sense of unhappiness.

The unpleasant aspects of doing business certainly took their toll. At one point Bento had a great deal of trouble extracting payment from a man named Anthony Alvares. After several months of enduring Alvares's shenanigans, Bento appealed to the city officials, and Alvares was arrested. Informed that he would not be released until he settled his debt, Alvares gamely asked Bento to meet with him so that they could make arrangements. But when Bento came for their scheduled meeting, Alvares physically attacked him.

With surprising calm, Bento remained willing to negotiate with his attacker. Even more surprising is that in the agreement that the two men reached, Bento agreed to cover the costs of the arrest and imprisonment—fees that were normally the responsibility of the guilty party. But Bento had not yet seen the end of Alvares's spite. Bento left the meeting to get the money for the arrest and imprisonment fees, and when he returned, he found Alvares's brother Gabriel waiting for him, poised for attack. For the second time that day, blows rained upon Bento's head. Gabriel then took Bento's hat, threw it in the gutter, and stepped on it—an especially insulting act at a time when hats symbolized a man's social status and identity.

Even at this point, Bento remained calm and willing to negotiate. The agreement that he and Alvares eventually reached stipulated that Bento would receive full payment of the original debt, compensation for losses he might have suffered from not being paid on time, and money to replace his hat. A bit hardened this time around, Bento refused to cover the costs of the arrest and imprisonment himself—but in an almost otherworldly display of kindheartedness, he agreed to lend Alvares the money to cover those fees. There is no record to show that Bento ever received any of the money that he was owed.

Bento's quiet self-assurance and equanimity served him in good stead his entire life. He was destined to endure more than his share of hostility and unfairness. On the other hand, he lacked the hard-edged grit that makes for success in business. He despised quarrels, and when he faced a conflict, his instinctive reaction was to yield, even at a cost to himself, rather than fight for his position. Bento's personality was not especially suited to the line of work he had inherited, and he knew it.

He also knew that he was growing less enthusiastic about the rewards of business life. Success as a merchant meant wealth, honor, and physical pleasure. It meant a home full of Turkish rugs and Chinese porcelain, deferential nods of the head on public streets, membership in committees that shaped civic life. But all of this left Bento cold. A few years later, looking back at this period, he wrote that his experience had taught him "the hollowness and futility of everything that is ordinarily encountered in daily life."

A major problem with basing happiness on wealth, honor, and physical pleasure, Bento realized, is that attaining them is so often out of our control. Merchants who pursue wealth above all things, for example, find their ability to achieve happiness compromised by any number of worries. Will suppliers keep their promises? Will shipments

COMMERCIAL BUILDINGS: As a merchant, Spinoza would have frequented Amsterdam's commodities exchange [above] and the Waag, or weighing house [below], which ensured the uniformity of weights.

View of the Rokin, Exchange in Amsterdam (Het Rockin, Mette Beurs), etching by Reinier Zeeman, mid-seventeenth century. Yale University Art Gallery.

View of the Weighing House De Waag, Amsterdam (Le Waag: Poids de la ville d'Amsterdam), etching by Maxime Lalanne, nineteenth century. Yale University Art Gallery.

survive storms or looting at sea? Will buyers be willing to offer good prices? With almost no power to influence those factors, the merchant spends life on an unsettling roller coaster of emotions. The pursuit of public admiration is just as problematic. People engaged in this pursuit have no control over their lives because they must shape themselves according to the fickle likes and dislikes of the audience whose esteem they are trying to win. For instance, they may need to dress according to the latest fashion or maintain a lavish household, even if neither particularly appeals to them. Even worse, they may find themselves supporting popular ideas that they do not truly believe.

Bento knew that he wanted a more permanent and consistent kind of happiness. He desired, he later wrote, "a true good, one which was capable of communicating itself and could alone affect the mind to the exclusion of all else . . . something whose discovery and acquisition would afford me a continuous and supreme joy to all eternity." Achieving this happiness would have to depend entirely on factors within Bento's control. He did not want the quality of his life to depend upon the ups and downs of chance or upon the whims of others.

Bento may not have thought of himself as a philosopher during the years that he worked as a merchant, but he was already doing the kind of thinking that philosophers do. He was asking one of the major questions that have preoccupied philosophers for centuries: What is it that leads to true happiness, that makes one's life good or worthwhile? At this point, all that Bento knew for certain was that he would need to search on his own for the answer.

CHAPTER NINE

MORE ATTEMPTS AT JEWISH ANSWERS

OF COURSE, IN THE MIDST OF BENTO'S NEW
reflections about happiness, he had not forgotten
the questions he had begun to consider at Talmud
Torah. Those gnawing questions about God, the
Bible, and the soul had not gone away, and Bento
must have continued to think about them whenever
he found the time. He may have still held onto the
hope that he would find his answers within the
Jewish tradition.

With work consuming so much of his time,
steady rabbinical study at Talmud Torah was out of
the question. Fortunately, Bento had other options.
The Nation ensured that men of all occupations
could study the Torah on a daily basis. In the
evenings, Bento attended classes at one of the most
highly respected of these programs, Rabbi Mortera's
Keter Torah. The curriculum focused primarily on

the Bible and its commentaries but also included forays into Jewish law and Jewish philosophy. Bento had the opportunity to study the ideas of Rabbi Moses ben Maimon, also known as Maimonides, one of the colossal figures in the history of Jewish thought. Maimonides was born in Spain during the twelfth century but spent the latter part of his life in Egypt.

Maimonides was a rationalist, a firm believer in the conclusions of logical thinking, and he asserted that there was no real contradiction between those conclusions and the Bible. Even the parts of the Bible that seem at first glance to make little sense are actually compatible with reason if only one approaches the biblical text with the proper understanding. This sometimes means differentiating between the times when biblical passages should be understood literally and the times when biblical passages should be understood figuratively. Read properly, the Bible presents scientific and philosophic truth, and this could not be otherwise, since the Bible is the word of God, and God is the very source of truth. And since the Bible presents only the truth, any scientific or philosophic assertion that contradicts the biblical text is by definition false.

As part of his project to demonstrate the perfect compatibility of religion and reason, Maimonides explained religious concepts in nonmagical, or naturalistic, terms. For instance, he rejected the

popular view of reward and punishment as a
system in which good people get prizes and bad
people get penalties. Instead, he viewed reward and
punishment as natural outgrowths of the activities
to which one devotes one's life. For Maimonides, the
best life is devoted to acquiring knowledge, and the
reward of the person who lives this best life is the
knowledge that has been acquired. Similarly, the
punishment of someone who fails to live that kind of
life is, quite simply, his or her lack of knowledge.

Maimonides also favored a naturalistic view
of God. He spoke harshly against the uneducated
masses whose conception of God is based on
anthropomorphism, the assigning of human
traits to something that is not human. In the
anthropomorphic view, God is a kind of superman
with the psychological, emotional, and even physical
life of human beings, only bigger and better.
Anthropomorphism is encouraged by the biblical

text, which refers, for instance, to God's hand or arm or satisfaction or fury. But reading such biblical references literally, according to Maimonides, is childishly simpleminded.

Maimonides's own conception of God draws heavily on the concept of a "prime mover" developed by the ancient Greek philosopher Aristotle. The prime mover is the original and eternal source of motion that is in itself unmoved or unaffected by anything else. According to this concept, any movement we observe in our world is part of a long causal chain. At the very end of the chain we might observe, for example, dirt stirring because of a fallen apple. We can then trace that movement back through the ever greater forces that caused it: the swaying branch that caused that apple to fall, the blustering wind that caused that branch to sway, and so on. For Maimonides, who followed the astronomical assumptions of his day, this "so on" involved a series of concentrically nesting heavenly spheres that surrounded the Earth. The blustering wind was caused by motion in the sphere closest to Earth, which was in turn caused by motion in the neighboring sphere, and so on throughout the spheres. To us it may seem extravagant to link something as trifling as the movement of dirt to the grand motions of the heavens, but this link seemed perfectly natural in an age when everything was understood to play a role in a comprehensive divine plan. Ultimately, the chain of motion reached all the way back to its source in the prime mover, the mover that was itself unmoved, which, for Maimonides, was God.

In the writings of this medieval Jewish thinker, Bento had finally found a fellow spirit. Maimonides's defense of reason and his exaltation of the intellectual life resonated with Bento's scholarly leanings. Maimonides's view of reward and punishment as natural outgrowths of people's choices harmonized beautifully with Bento's doubts about an afterlife in which God metes out final judgment. And Maimonides's naturalistic view of God as prime mover was far more convincing than the magical, superhuman character in which so many people seemed to believe so naïvely.

But Bento was never one to accept another person's ideas whole. As he sifted through Maimonides's views, he realized that he had several objections. First, if Maimonides's God is the source of the world's motion, is it really necessary to think that God occupies a separate sphere above and beyond the natural world? Perhaps God is simply the force of nature itself, internal to the world we know. Furthermore, to maintain the equivalence of truth derived from reason and truth derived from the Bible, Maimonides had to claim that the prophets were the greatest of thinkers. After all, the prophets had received the word of God in its purest and most direct form, and by Maimonides's standards, that word was none other than the highest form of reason. But even a cursory look at the Bible reveals that many prophets were simple, uneducated people, often with rather primitive views of the world around them.

Bento had already learned to keep his views to himself, and this remained his policy at Keter Torah. As far as anyone could see, Bento was a model Jew. He was engaging in religious study, observing the period of mourning for his father, attending synagogue services, and making regular contributions to community funds. He showed every sign of becoming a pillar of the Nation, just as his father had been before him. But in the unspoken views he was developing about the immortality of the soul, the nature of God, and the truth of the Bible, Bento was already an outsider. He would never be able to return to the mainstream views of his community.

It was fascinating, really. Bento was living the double life that was so much a part of his community's history—looking and acting like one thing on the outside but being something quite different on the inside. But Bento was living this life in reverse. The Judaism that the Portuguese crypto-Jews had so devotedly protected in their private, inner lives was more and more the false exterior that Bento showed the world.

CHAPTER TEN

EXPLORING THE
WIDER WORLD

THERE WAS ONE ASPECT OF BEING A MERCHANT
that Bento loved, and that was his contact with
the intellectual world outside the Nation. He was
learning about recent developments in science,
math, philosophy, and politics, and he was also
discovering that many non-Jews, too, were asking
questions about their religious traditions.

A number of Bento's new acquaintances were
Collegiants, members of a Protestant group that
held Sunday meetings, which they called "colleges,"
for a combination of worship and study. The
Collegiants disliked highly organized structures
of leadership and elaborate codes of belief. They
believed in a simple form of Christianity based
on the basic truths that Jesus had taught: the
importance of loving God and of loving other
people. Beyond the basics, individuals could believe,

practice, and interpret the Bible as they chose. At their Sunday meetings, group members took turns offering their own understandings of biblical texts and exchanged a wide variety of opinions.

Bento was not interested in becoming a Christian. Even the Collegiants held fairly traditional views about the immortality of the soul and about the Bible as the literal word of God, and those were ideas that Bento could no longer accept. But he agreed wholeheartedly that true religion is based on the simple moral foundation of loving other people and loving God, and he frequently joined the Collegiants' Sunday meetings.

Bento's forays into the non-Jewish world also brought him into some very impressive bookstores. Amsterdam's high degree of tolerance enabled local printers to produce books considered too controversial elsewhere. Authors from all over Europe flocked to the city to have their work published, and the city was full of books that were not openly available in the rest of Europe.

But at the same time that Bento learned of the exhilarating wealth of books just a short step away from home, he became aware of a serious personal limitation. He was unable to read Latin. Since antiquity, Latin had been the dominant language of European scholarship. To make any real intellectual

MENNONITE CHURCH: Many of the Collegiants were Mennonites who worshiped in simple sanctuaries. Mennonites rejected infant baptism, believing instead that individuals could join the church only when they were mature enough to do so of their own accord. Mennonites also advocated the separation of church and state.

De Kerk der Mennonisten De Son genaemt, engraving from Casparus Commelin's *Beschryvinge van Amsterdam,* 1694. Image courtesy of the Getty's Open Content Program, Getty Research Institute.

BOOKSTORES:

Amsterdam bookstores were often operated by Huguenots, or French Protestants, many of whom fled to the Dutch Republic to avoid persecution. These booksellers were also publishers, and some of them produced books that were banned in other countries.

Devant de la Bource d'Amsterdam (In front of the Amsterdam Stock Exchange) from Johannes Phoonsen and Jean Pierre Ricard (trans.), *Les Loix et les Coutumes du Change des Principales Places de l'Europe* (Amsterdam: Estienne Roger, 1715). Rare Book Collection, Lillian Goldman Law Library, Yale Law School.

progress outside the Jewish community, Bento's first task would be to learn it.

There were certainly many people in the Nation who knew Latin. When they had been living as crypto-Jews in Portugal, many of them had attended Catholic universities where knowledge of that language was essential. But there was no formal Latin instruction in the Jewish community, so Bento had to seek instruction elsewhere. He eventually found his way to a colorful character named Franciscus van den Enden. In his home on one of Amsterdam's major canals, Van den Enden ran a school to prepare students for university. Classes focused on Latin as well as on the basic texts upon which any subsequent studies would build.

Van den Enden was an excellent teacher, and he attracted many students from merchant families uninterested in the public Latin school run by Calvinists. He was not particularly religious, although as a very young man he had been connected with the Jesuit order, an organization of priests at the forefront of the Catholic Church's attempt to combat the Protestant Reformation. Van den Enden had studied at various Jesuit schools and at one point had even planned to become a priest. But the young man's conduct did not meet the approval of his superiors. He was twice kicked out of the order, and he eventually gave up his plans for the priesthood. He married and had children, and he supported himself and his family primarily through teaching. For a brief stint he also ran an art gallery and bookshop. He was a great fan of the dramatic arts and had written a play.

Van den Enden was a highly educated man and a courageous thinker. In the context of his day and age, one of his most unusual ideas was that girls deserve a good education. He happily accepted female students, and he made sure that his own daughter, Clara Maria, had the same opportunities as the boys he was teaching. Eventually Clara Maria even became a teacher at his school. Girls also participated fully in the production of the plays that were a central part of the curriculum. At the time it was widely considered inappropriate for girls and women to act in the theater, and female parts were generally played by boys whose voices had not yet deepened.

Bento's new teacher also had some surprising political and religious views. Van den Enden's ideal government was a democracy in which well-educated citizens, both men and women, elected officials for limited terms and settled disagreements by majority vote. This government would be kept separate from religion, which Van den Enden considered an entirely private matter. Citizens would enjoy complete freedom to think and believe as they pleased, and they would also be guaranteed absolute freedom of speech. The Dutch Republic was still far from Van den Enden's ideal, but it came closer than any other place in Europe, and Van den Enden loved his country.

Bento must have been enthralled by this profoundly independent and exuberant thinker. Van den Enden was never one to be deterred by social or religious convention, and he took great delight in his reputation among the *predikanten* as a corrupter of youth. His energy was boundless, and even his death, twenty years after Bento attended his school, was dramatic. At the age of 72, just when most people would be settling into a calm old age, he joined a plot to assassinate King Louis XIV of France, whose army had invaded Van den Enden's beloved Dutch Republic. Van den Enden was caught and hanged.

Bento's studies with Van den Enden, his participation in Collegiant circles, his visits to city bookstores, and his general exposure to the vibrancy of Amsterdam added an exciting new dimension to his life. Enriched by his traditional background in Judaism, these varied elements were the raw materials from which Bento was already beginning to construct a highly original and unified system of thought—a philosophy—of his own.

CHAPTER ELEVEN

THE SUSPECTED
HERETIC

NO ONE REALLY KNOWS EXACTLY WHAT SET OFF THE alarm among the Portuguese Jews in Amsterdam. Perhaps it was Bento's increasing involvement in the outside world. The Nation's many merchants maintained business connections with non-Jews, and a smaller but significant number of Jews enjoyed social and intellectual relationships outside the Jewish community. But the nature of Bento's involvement seemed different. Bento was not just dipping his feet into that world. He was diving in altogether.

Or perhaps Bento was becoming careless about his observance of Jewish laws and traditions. It may be that he skipped services from time to time at the synagogue or that even when he showed up, he was just going through the motions, mouthing empty words or daydreaming as he held his neglected prayer book in his hands. Perhaps he was spotted eating food at a non-kosher establishment or engaging in an activity prohibited on the Sabbath. But then again, Bento would not have been alone in this kind of indiscretion. Rabbi Mortera and the other rabbis of the community were constantly railing against individuals whose religious observance seemed wanting.

Maybe Bento had begun to express his views more openly. He might have slipped simply because his ideas were raging too furiously to remain suppressed. Or he might have become quite deliberate in revealing his views. He was an earnest seeker after truth, unafraid to look straight in the face the ideas that others found dangerous or unpleasant, and his very personality militated against the dishonesty of a double life. Furthermore, as the Alvares incident suggests, Bento was a sincere believer—perhaps to the point of naïveté—in the reasonableness of other people. He might have revealed some of his insights in a genuine attempt to involve others in a shared quest for the truth. There would also have been a less flattering but very human motivation for speaking his mind. Bento was young, smart, and self-confident. It must have been tempting to demonstrate, with his own sharp reasoning, the flaws in views that he could no longer accept.

Another student at Keter Torah might have encouraged Bento to express himself more freely. This student was Juan de Prado, a Spanish crypto-Jew who had recently arrived in Amsterdam and was taking advantage of the opportunity to learn more about his religion. But Prado was not at all convinced by many of the Jewish ideas he was encountering for the first time. His questions and doubts, like Bento's, fell into three major categories: the nature of God, the authorship and authority of the Bible, and the immortality of the soul. Prado and Bento soon realized that their thoughts on these issues were moving in much the same direction.

It did not take long for Prado to gain a reputation for his problematic views. According to the testimony that was later gathered, Prado not only engaged in "scandalous actions" such as mocking Jews on their way to the synagogue and belittling community officials but also announced that certain activities prohibited by Jewish law were actually permissible. Perhaps Prado also aired some indiscreet ideas in class. If this was the case, Bento might have felt driven to make his own eyebrow-raising contributions to the discussion. An early historian of the Amsterdam Jewish community, Daniel Levi de Barrios, later wrote about the conflict that developed in Rabbi Mortera's classes. Mortera, according to de Barrios, bravely fought

"in the defense of religion and against atheism."
The historian went on to present a somewhat
fanciful description of the opposition that Mortera
faced: "*Thorns* [in Spanish, *Espinos*] are they that,
in the *Fields* [*Prados*] of impiety, aim to shine
with the fire that consumes them." De Barrios's
Spanish vocabulary ensured the obviousness of his
references to Bento de Spinoza and Juan de Prado.

Though we can't know for certain how it came
to be, Bento's radical views were seeping out. People
were beginning to wonder and whisper. Could the
rumors be true? Michael Spinoza had been such a
respected member of the Nation, selflessly devoting
his time, effort, and money to community causes.
And he had been a good, loving father as well.
Could Michael's son really be going so far astray? It
was one thing to slip here and there in one's beliefs
or practices, but it sounded as though Bento were
doing more than that. He was turning out to be—
and this was so horrifying that it was practically
unthinkable—an atheist. Atheists were malicious
and sinful, and everyone knew that they belonged
in hell. Something had to be done, and quickly,
to save Bento's soul and prevent the spread of his
contamination.

Shock soon turned to anger. How could Bento
spit in the faces of the people he had known all his
life—and not only spit in their faces but potentially

enrage the Dutch authorities and risk everything the Nation had worked so hard to establish? For one person thinking along these lines, the anger built up until it erupted in a brutal physical attack. As Bento was exiting a public building—a synagogue or a theater, it seems—a Jewish man armed with a knife savagely charged at him. Bento was left physically unharmed but emotionally shaken. His coat had been gashed by the blade, and Bento was convinced that the man had intended to kill him. Bento never repaired or threw away the damaged coat. It served him his entire life as a potent reminder of the dangers of intolerance.

The attacker was probably acting independently, but Bento was already a source of unease for the entire Jewish community. To confirm whether the nasty rumors were true, two young members of the Nation approached Bento, claiming that they were eager to hear his opinions so that they could clear up their own religious doubts. They assured Bento that he had nothing to fear in speaking freely with them, since they, like him, were in honest pursuit of the truth. Bento found the appeal irresistible. He imprudently let down his guard and gave earnest and heartfelt answers to the two men's questions about such issues as the immortality of the soul and the nature of God. The men were so scandalized by Bento's blatant disregard for traditional Jewish thought that they first supposed he was joking.

As he spoke with the two men, Bento grew increasingly suspicious of their motives. He ended the conversation as soon as he could, but the inquisition had already begun. The two men promptly made public what they had heard, and soon the entire Nation knew that Bento had broken completely and deliberately from Jewish tradition. He denied the immortality of the soul, he rejected the truth of the Bible as the actual word of God, and he believed in God "only philosophically." What that last thing meant was not entirely clear, but it seemed to indicate, at the very least, that Bento's God did not especially care about people or make any particular demands on human behavior. The rumors were true, then: Bento really had reached the unthinkable point of atheism.

Infuriated by the report, Rabbi Mortera rushed to Bento, urging him to abandon his evil opinions and return faithfully to Jewish belief. Bento was a promising young man from a good family, and if he were only willing to spend more time poring over Jewish texts, he might find answers to his satisfaction. Bento's sharp mind and intellectual bent suggested that he could even have a brilliant career as a rabbi. The rabbi also added a threat. If

Bento did not comply immediately, he would face *cherem.*

Rabbi Mortera might well have felt a righteous indignation as he set out to vanquish evil. But the reality turned out to be far less comforting. Unmoved by the rabbi's dire threat and spurred on by relief at dropping all pretense, Bento responded with an arrogance for which he was not usually known. As one of his early biographers wrote, Bento answered that he "knew the gravity" of Rabbi Mortera's threats, and that "in return for the trouble" which Rabbi Mortera had taken to teach him the Hebrew language, Bento was "quite willing to show him how to excommunicate."

CHAPTER TWELVE

EXCOMMUNICATION

BY THIS POINT, A BREAK BETWEEN BENTO AND THE
Nation seemed inevitable. But the Portuguese Jews
were reluctant to give up on a young man who
had grown up in their midst with such promise.
Bento's business was not doing well, and perhaps
he could be lured by money. With the Nation's many
successful merchants, it was relatively easy to come
by a sum that just might tempt the young man into
obedience. One thousand guilders seemed about
right. The weekly wage of a skilled worker was just
under three guilders, and the annual stipend of
a schoolteacher was about two hundred guilders.
Officials of the Nation approached Bento with the
enticing offer.

Bento would hear nothing of it. He would refuse
even ten times that amount. He was uninterested in
wealth, and he was uninterested in appearances. He

DECLARATION OF CHEREM: This Portuguese text was recorded in the *Escamoth*, the Nation's register of community resolutions and regulations. At the actual ceremony in the synagogue, the declaration was made in Hebrew.

Ban against Spinoza recorded in the *Escamoth* of the Jewish community Talmud Torah, 1656, Stadsarchief Amsterdam.

cared for truth, and truth only. There was only one thing left for the Jewish community to do.

Bento was twenty-three years old when his excommunication became official on July 27, 1656. At the fearful ceremony, in the synagogue filled to its capacity, an official of the Nation read the biting declaration of *cherem*. The text used Bento's Hebrew name, Baruch, as well as a variant of his family name, Espinoza, and began with a brief history:

> *The Lords of the* ma'amad *[the synagogue's governing committee], having long known of the evil opinions and acts of Baruch de Spinoza, have endeavored by various means and promises, to turn him from his evil ways. But having failed to make him mend his wicked ways, and, on the contrary, daily receiving more and more serious information about the abominable heresies which he practiced and taught and about his monstrous deeds, and having for this numerous trustworthy witnesses who have deposed and born [sic] witness to this effect in the presence of the said Espinoza, they became convinced of the truth of this matter; and after all of this has been investigated in the presence of the honorable* chachamim *[religious authorities], they have decided, with their consent, that the said Espinoza should be*

excommunicated and expelled from the people of Israel.

Then came the actual declaration of *cherem*:

> *By decree of the angels and by the command of the holy men, we excommunicate, expel, curse and damn Baruch de Espinoza, with the consent of God, Blessed be He, and with the consent of the entire holy congregation, and in front of these holy scrolls with the 613 precepts which are written therein. . . .*

Next was a staggering series of curses, some of which were based on biblical stories. Never before had the Nation unleashed such ferocity against any of its members:

> *[We curse] him with the excommunication with which Joshua banned Jericho and with the curse which Elisha cursed the boys and with all the castigations that are written in the Book of the Law. Cursed be he by day and cursed be he by night; cursed be he when he lies down and cursed be he when he rises up. Cursed be he when he goes out and cursed be he when he comes in. The Lord will not spare him, but then the anger of the Lord and his jealousy shall*

smoke against that man, and all the curses that are written in this book shall lie upon him, and the Lord shall blot out his name from under heaven. And the Lord shall separate him unto evil out of all the tribes of Israel, according to all the curses of the covenant that are written in this book of the law. But you that cleave unto the Lord your God are alive every one of you this day.

Finally came the specifics about how the Jewish community, including Bento's closest relatives, should relate to the outcast:

[N]o one should communicate with him, neither in writing, nor accord him any favor nor stay with him under the same roof nor come within four cubits in his vicinity; nor shall he read any treatise composed or written by him.

Completely absent in this exceptionally severe *cherem* was the usual opportunity for the sinner to repent and be readmitted into Jewish life. The Jews of Amsterdam had barred their doors, their hearts, and their minds against the outcast. As far as the Nation was concerned, Bento had simply ceased to exist.

Bento's *cherem* was the harshest one ever issued by the Jews of Amsterdam, and the reason for its unusual harshness remains a mystery. The *cherem* declaration itself is notoriously silent about the specifics. Particularly puzzling is that the Nation's other prominent heretics during the first half of the 1600s, Uriel da Costa and Juan de Prado, were not subjected to anything even approaching the fury and finality of Bento's *cherem*. Da Costa, who had enraged the Nation with his rejection of rabbinic authority and the soul's immortality, was excommunicated not once but twice, and even after his second *cherem* he was given the chance to rejoin the community.

Prado was an even closer parallel to Bento. The men were friends, and they held the same unacceptable views. The joint reference to *espinos* and *prados* in de Barrios's history of the Nation— and de Barrios was not the only one to use these puns—suggests that scandals surrounding the two men were seen by the Nation as a single chapter in its history. But the community's reactions to the two men were markedly different.

Prado was treated far more gently. Around the time of Bento's excommunication, Prado was issued a stern warning about his own precarious position, and he compliantly made a public apology in the synagogue. Nonetheless, Prado continued to offend

SCENE OF THE *CHEREM*: This illustration depicts the interior of the Talmud Torah synagogue, where Spinoza's *cherem* was formally declared.

Interior of the Portuguese Synagogue on the Houtgracht in Amsterdam, attributed to Jan Veenhuysen, 1664. Collection Rijksmuseum, Amsterdam.

the community, and two years later, the Nation declared a *cherem* against him. The declaration used Prado's Hebrew name, Daniel:

> *Since Daniel de Prado has been convicted by various witnesses before the* Senhores *of the* ma'amad *of having reverted very scandalously, of having desired anew to seduce different people with his detestable opinions against our Holy Law, the* Senhores *of the* ma'amad, *with the advice of the rabbis, have decided unanimously that the said Daniel de Prado should be excommunicated and separated from the nation. By the threat of the same excommunication, they order that no member of this Holy Community should communicate with him, neither verbally nor in writing, neither in this city nor outside it, with the exception of the members of his family. May God spare his people from evil, and peace be upon Israel.*

The difference between this declaration and the one used in Bento's case can hardly be more apparent. Aside from the references to Prado's "having reverted very scandalously" to his ways and to his "detestable opinions," the text is a matter-of-fact statement of the situation and its consequences. Completely absent are the rage and indignation exhibited in the heap of curses hurled at Bento. Also absent is the totality of the expulsion. Prado's relatives were still allowed to maintain contact with him, while Bento's relatives—including even his brother Gabriel, with whom Bento was running the family business—were not. Furthermore, the Nation showed a sensitivity toward Prado that was completely lacking in Bento's case. Despite the declaration that "no member of this Holy Community" should communicate with Prado, "neither in this city nor outside it," the leaders of the Nation, as it turned out, offered to help him relocate to another Jewish community overseas.

If Bento and Prado were expelled from the Jewish community for the same offenses, why was Bento's sentence so much heavier? Unless new historical evidence is discovered, there will probably never be a completely satisfactory answer to this question. One interesting idea to consider, however, is that Bento was a child of the Nation in ways that Prado—and da Costa, for that matter—was not. Da Costa and Prado had spent their formative years in Spain or Portugal, and both men had only recently arrived in Amsterdam when they began expressing views contrary to Jewish tradition. It would have been no surprise, then, that their understanding of Judaism was incomplete and frequently mistaken. Their knowledge of their own traditions was based on a hodgepodge of distant memories and a handful of surviving practices, and for years they had needed to keep even this diminished Jewish identity hidden beneath a Christian exterior.

But Bento's life was a different story altogether. Bento had never had to navigate the religious minefields of Spain and Portugal. He had spent his entire life in an astonishingly tolerant city, in a proud Jewish community that was the marvel and envy of Jews throughout Europe. As a newborn baby, he was openly welcomed into the Jewish community in his circumcision and naming ceremony. He would never have to fear the permanent bodily sign of his Jewishness, and he would never need to keep his Hebrew name a secret. As a schoolchild, he had received a comprehensive Jewish education. He would never have to feel the inadequacy of his parents' and grandparents' generations, with their sadly limited knowledge of Hebrew and Judaism. As an adult, he had access to everything that made Jewish life possible—synagogues, holy books, classes, ritual items, kosher meat. He would never need to live a limited and makeshift Judaism without those necessities. Bento was a native, blessed son. To his fellow Jews, those who had sacrificed so much to ease the way for him, Bento's unacceptable actions and beliefs must have felt like a profound betrayal.

And how did Bento respond to the Nation's unforgiving declaration against him? He apparently did not answer the community's summons to the synagogue and so was not even present at the dark and dreadful ceremony. When a messenger brought him the news, he had only this to say: "All the better; they do not force me to do anything that I would not have done of my own accord if I did not dread scandal; but, since they want it that way, I enter gladly on the path that is opened to me, with the consolation that my departure will be more innocent than was the exodus of the early Hebrews from Egypt."

Bento was making his own exodus with an absolutely clear conscience. He could not have failed to note the irony. He was fulfilling the requirement set down by the ancient rabbis that he had so enthusiastically recited at the *seder* in his younger years: *In every generation, one is obligated to think of oneself as having personally left Egypt.* But Bento was doing just the reverse of what the rabbis had intended. The rabbis' Promised Land, the world of devotion to Jewish texts, ideas, and traditions, had become for Bento an Egypt, a land of narrowness and oppression. Bento was making his own journey into freedom. His own Promised Land was still uncharted, but he was determined to find it.

There was another reversal. The direst and most bloodcurdling curses imaginable had just been hurled at a young man whose name meant "blessed" in both Portuguese and Hebrew. But Bento was unperturbed. He shed his identities as Bento and Baruch and bravely set out to find new blessings of his own. It was probably at Van den Enden's school that he had first learned the Latin word "benedictus," which he now adopted as his first name. His new name, just like his old ones, meant "blessed."

PART TWO

A Pioneering Outcast

CHAPTER THIRTEEN

LENSES AND
THE NEW SCIENCE

SPINOZA'S NEWFOUND FREEDOM WAS ALMOST dizzying, but there were practical matters that required immediate attention. First he needed to find new lodgings. Under the terms of the *cherem*, his younger brother Gabriel could not continue sharing a home with him, and staying in the Jewish neighborhood was out of the question because of the unpleasant situations that would arise. Second, he needed to find a new means of support. Gabriel could no longer work as his partner, and Spinoza was perfectly happy to leave the family business to him.

Spinoza solved both problems by taking lodgings with Van den Enden. Not only could he continue his own studies but he could also instruct Van den Enden's beginning students in order to cover the expenses of his room and board. It is also possible that a romantic interest kept Spinoza dedicated to Van den Enden's school. According to one account of Spinoza's life during this period, the young man fell deeply in love with Van den Enden's daughter, Clara Maria, who was remarkable for the sharpness of her mind and her mastery of Latin and music. Spinoza wanted to marry the accomplished young woman, but much to his dismay, he found that he had a rival among Van den Enden's students. The other student won. The two suitors were equals in terms of their personal charms, but the other man was able to offer, in addition, the gift of a pearl necklace. The gift clinched the proposal, and Clara Maria's heart was conquered.

Whether or not the story is true, Spinoza was certainly in no position to purchase pearl necklaces or any other luxuries. It was essential for him to supplement his income from Van den Enden, and he quickly found himself a trade, one especially suited to his taste and temperament. He decided to become a lens grinder.

Lens grinding was solitary work that demanded total concentration, abundant patience, and strict discipline—a perfect combination for Spinoza's quiet, thoughtful, and intense personality. Craftsmen had shaped crude lenses from polished crystal since ancient times, but glass lenses as we know them did not emerge in Europe until the end of the thirteenth century. The earliest glass lenses functioned primarily as magnifying glasses, but eyeglasses had already begun to appear by the 1300s. The invention of the microscope and the telescope in the early 1600s suddenly gave the humble lens many new and increasingly sophisticated applications.

By Spinoza's day, lens-grinding lathes existed in various shapes and sizes. Smaller lathes sat on tabletops and were powered by a hand-turned crank while larger models stood on the floor and were powered by a foot pedal. In either case, a series of wheels, pulleys, and shafts transferred the lens grinder's hand or foot movements to a rotating wheel. The craftsman fastened to this wheel a cupped grinding mold designed for the specific lens he was making. The lens began as a blank, an unground piece of glass in approximately the desired size, which the lens grinder usually purchased from a supplier. After affixing a handle to the blank, the craftsman held it against the cupped grinding mold, which rotated along with the wheel to which it was attached. With the craftsman's application of subtle pressure at just the right points, the grinding cup filed off tiny particles of glass until the lens took on the grinding cup's shape. Because the work was slow and physically tiring—even the simplest lens might take an hour to grind, and more complicated lenses took far longer—some lens grinders developed

mechanical devices to keep the blank in place. Spinoza, however, insisted on holding the blank himself, claiming that "a free hand yields safer and better results than any machine."

The physical work was grounded in an intellectually fascinating foundation.

For centuries, lens grinding had been little more than a trial-and-error activity, but by the mid-1600s, the craft was being completely transformed by the brand-new field of optics, which examines the properties of light and its interactions with different forms of matter. Lenses for different purposes required all sorts of adjustments in materials and equipment, not to mention complex mathematical calculations to determine size and curvature. Spinoza immersed himself in both the craft and the science of his newfound trade.

LENS GRINDING: Spinoza may have used a lathe similar to the one in this illustration.

Woodcut from *L'occhiale all'occhio, dioptrica pratica* by Carlo Antonio Manzini (Bologna: Herede del Benacci, 1660). Bernard Becker Medical Library, Washington University School of Medicine.

For the ever-curious Spinoza, however, the real thrill of lens grinding lay in its contribution to the incredible transformations taking place throughout the world of science. Nowadays we are used to the concept of the scientific method. We assume that scientists formulate hypotheses based on observation of the natural world, and we expect those hypotheses to be subjected to careful experimentation before they are accepted as true. And for us, mathematics is an obvious means of validating a scientific claim. But observation, experimentation, and mathematics did not serve as foundations of scientific knowledge until well into the seventeenth century. Before then, science was based largely on traditional beliefs that strike us today as little more than myths or fairy tales.

The force of gravity, for instance, was once understood as an object's almost mystical attempt to return to its place of origin. According to the traditional view, the world was composed of four elements—earth, air, fire, and water—and each of these elements had a home to which it constantly wanted to return. The center of the Earth was the home of the element earth, for instance, while the heavens were the home of the element fire. A rock, composed of the element earth, fell to the ground because it was trying to return to the center of the Earth, while a candle's flame, composed of fire, rose into the air because it was trying to return to the heavens. Specific objects were believed to fall at different speeds because they contained various combinations of the four basic elements, each one striving to go somewhere else.

The study of the cosmos was also shaped by mythlike views, the same set of time-honored ideas that influenced Maimonides. The universe was finite, and at its exact center was the unmoving Earth, composed of the four elements. Surrounding the Earth was a fifth element, ether, which was found only in the heavens and was not subject to the changes or imperfections of the four earthly elements. The ethereal region was the home of the moon, the sun, the planets, and the stars, which were contained within a series of concentrically nesting spheres—spheres because the heavens were assumed to be perfect, and the sphere was considered the most perfect of shapes, with all points on its surface equidistant from its center. These heavenly spheres turned in perfect movements that were first put into motion by the prime mover, itself unmoved by anything else.

These sorts of traditional notions did reflect a crude sort of science. Ancient people saw that the natural world is composed of different kinds of materials that behave in different ways. They observed that fire invariably rises upward while a

Artes múdi funt quatuor·ignis·aer·aqua·terra· qua/
rum haec eſt natura.Ignis tenuis acutus ac mobilis.
Aer mobilis acutus & craſſus. Aqua craſſa obtuſa
& mobilis.Terra craſſa obtuſa immobilis. Quae &iam ita ſibi
inuicem cómiſcétur. Terra quidem craſſa obtuſa & immobilis
cum aquae craſſitudine & obtuſitate conligatur.Deinde aqua
aeri in craſſitudine & mobilitate coniungitur.Rurſus aer igni
communione acute & mobili conligatur.Terra autem et ignis
a ſe ſeparantur ſed a duobus mediis aque & aere iungunt. Nec
itaq; ne confuſa minus conligatur ſubiecta expreſſa ſunt figura

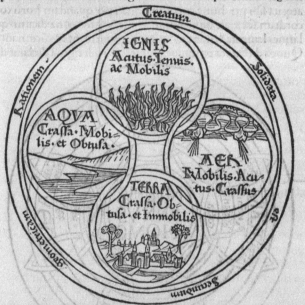

Ceterum ſanctus. Ambroſius hec eleméta per qualitates qbus
ſibi inuicem quadam nature communione cómiſcentur·ita his
verbis diſtinguit.Terra inquit arida & frigida eſt. Aqua frigi
da atq; humida eſt. Aer calidus & humidus.Ignis calidus eſt

feather and a sword fall downward but at different speeds. They felt a steady, unmoving earth beneath their feet at the same time that they saw the sun moving across the sky. In formulating their notions about gravity and the cosmos, ancient people were in fact doing one of the major things modern scientists do: they were looking at the natural world around them and attempting to find explanations that would account for all the phenomena they observed.

Nonetheless, there is something that today seems rather unscientific about these ancient notions: the assumption that physical objects possess a sort of soul. The traditional explanation of gravity, for instance, assumed that objects contain intelligent spirits that knowingly seek their natural homes. The traditional view of the cosmos assumed that the universe is guided by a godly perfection that finds expression in spherical structures, circular motion, and flawless ether. The traditional idea of the prime mover assumed a mystical force above and beyond all human understanding. Intelligent spirits, idealized guiding principles, and mystical powers are just not what we today consider science.

For thousands of years, this conceptual mingling of matter and spirit stood in the way of science. Spiritual qualities, whether or not they exist, are ultimately unknowable, and this means that wherever they were assumed to operate, scientific inquiry had to end. And since so much of what constituted each object was unknowable, it was impossible to draw connections between one object and another. It was impossible to see, for instance, that beneath external appearances, the same rules of gravity apply to both a feather and a stone.

In Spinoza's day, the old notions were gradually giving way to modern understandings. People curious about the workings of the natural world dropped objects from towers, rolled balls down inclines, observed the movements of planets, and never stopped measuring what they saw. From their observations and experiments, they began to construct new notions of how the world works. These people subscribed to empiricism, the idea that we arrive at knowledge through the evidence that our senses provide. Others moved in what was essentially the opposite direction. Less confident in our senses' ability to gather accurate information, these thinkers began by using the certain truths of mathematics to construct abstract models. Only then did they look to the real world for confirmation of what they had already determined. This second group subscribed to rationalism, the idea that accurate knowledge comes through the exercise of reason and logic, without the interference of sensory experience.

THE COSMOS: In this traditional depiction, Earth sits at the center, surrounded by the moon, the planets that are visible to the naked eye, the firmament of fixed stars, and the crystalline heavens, or the waters that God set above the firmament in the act of creation. The final two spheres are labeled "prime mover" and "empyrean heavens, habitat of God and of all the elect."

Diagram of the geocentric universe from *Cosmographia Petri Apiani* by Peter Apian and Frisius Gemma, 1574. General Collection, Beinecke Rare Book and Manuscript Library, Yale University.

The new approaches soon began to overturn the traditional ideas. In the first part of the seventeenth century, the Italian scientist Galileo Galilei dealt a serious blow to the old view of gravity by determining that objects of unequal weight fall with exactly the same speed in a vacuum. Galileo also attacked the old Earth-centered view of the cosmos by claiming that the Earth is just one part of a planetary system that orbits the sun. Christiaan Huygens, who later became a friend of Spinoza's, studied the rings of Saturn and discovered Saturn's moon Titan. Our moon, it turned out, is just one of many moons in the larger planetary system. The Dutch made especially impressive progress in biology, an area that had been replete with mystical notions connected to the supposed properties of the four elements. Antony van Leeuwenhoek, born just a month before Spinoza, discovered single-celled organisms, studied muscle fiber and bacteria, and observed blood flow in the tiniest capillaries. Jan Swammerdam, four years younger than Spinoza, was the first to see and describe red blood cells, and he understood for the first time that an egg, a larva, a pupa, and an adult insect are not four different creatures but distinct phases in the life of the same animal.

With the new focus on observation, experimentation, and mathematical reasoning, modern science was well on its way. But the traditional ideas did not vanish easily or quickly. For one thing, the old ideas had originated in ancient times and had been accepted as truth for so long that many people could not even imagine questioning them. Even more importantly, the old ideas bore the stamp of religious authority. They had predated Christianity, but they had had the backing of the Catholic Church for centuries, and they were accepted unquestioningly by most Protestants as well. Jews, too, generally assumed the truth of the traditional explanations. Spinoza would have encountered the Earth-centered view of the universe and the concept of a prime mover in his study of Maimonides.

There was much in the traditional explanations that was conducive to a religious worldview. Almost all Europeans of the seventeenth century, no matter what their religion, believed in a God who created everything, who continued to keep everything in existence, and who had a master plan for all of creation—in short, a God who was very much present in the universe. It was easy to see God's presence in things like the home-seeking spirits of objects, the all-embracing perfection of the universe, and the prime mover that sets everything else into motion. And with their mixing of matter and spirit, especially in relation to human beings, the old explanations upheld the religious notion of a soul. Over time the old explanations came to be viewed as absolutely essential to religious belief. The search for other explanations was readily seen as a denial of God's presence in the universe—an act of heresy.

The most famous example of religious resistance to the new science remains the case of Galileo. When Spinoza was just a few months old, the Catholic Church tried Galileo for heresy because of his belief in a sun-centered planetary system. The Church was furiously opposed to the sun-centered view for several reasons. First, if the Earth is simply one of several satellites revolving around the sun, the Earth and the people who inhabit it no longer hold a central position in the universe. The possibility that human beings are marginal and fairly insignificant in the greater scheme of the universe contrasted sharply with the traditional religious view in which man is the crowning glory of creation and God fashioned everything else on man's behalf. Second, the sun-centered view directly conflicts with various biblical passages, such as the story of Joshua making the sun stand still so that the ancient Israelites could finish a critical battle victoriously. If the Bible itself says that the sun moves and the Earth does not, who was man to say otherwise? Finally, there was simply a great deal of unease about human beings, with all their limitations and smallness, meddling in

F. Villamoena Fecit

GALILEO GALILEI: The inscription identifies Galileo as a philosopher, mathematician, and member of the Accademia dei Lincei ("Academy of the Lynxes"), an Italian scientific academy founded at the beginning of the seventeenth century. Since lynxes are known for their sharp vision, the Accademia's name reflected its devotion to the new science based on careful observation of the natural world.

Frontispiece by Francesco Villamena from *Opere di Galileo Galilei . . . In questa nuova editione insieme raccolte, e di varii trattati dell' istesso autore non piu stampati accresciute* (1655–1656). General Collection, Beinecke Rare Book and Manuscript Library, Yale University.

GALILEO'S ACHIEVEMENTS: In this illustration, the elderly Galileo presents a telescope to his three muses, Mathematics, Astronomy, and Optics. With his left hand he points to the sun-centered planetary system that he championed.

Illustration by Stefano Della Bella from *Opere di Galileo Galilei . . . In questa nuova editione insieme raccolte, e di varii trattati dell' istesso autore non piu stampati accresciute* (1655–1656). General Collection, Beinecke Rare Book and Manuscript Library, Yale University.

matters well beyond themselves. Inventions such as the telescope, which made it possible to explore parts of creation invisible to natural sight, did not give human beings the right to poke their pathetic little noses into the majestic workings of God.

The Church forced Galileo to make a public statement denouncing the sun-centered view and kept him under house arrest for the final nine years of his life. Galileo obeyed the Church's requirements and never again publicized any theories that violated official doctrine. But whether he actually gave up his view that the Earth revolves around the sun is another question. Shortly after his trial, he is said to have quietly uttered the famous words, "And yet it moves."

Galileo was not the only person who faced charges of heresy for his scientific conclusions, and the Catholic Church was not the only religious force that resisted the new science. As evidence accumulated, however, the new science gradually gained the upper hand, and religions had no choice but to accommodate fresh understandings of nature into their belief systems. The process took time. In Galileo's case, more than 120 years passed before the Church lifted its ban on books promoting the sun-centered view.

During Spinoza's lifetime, the war was still raging between religion and the new science, and the outcome remained uncertain. As a lens grinder, Spinoza was a modest but essential foot soldier in this war. It would take a substantial accumulation of raw evidence to overturn the old myths about nature, and the microscope and telescope were essential in this effort. And these two pieces of equipment relied on humble lens grinders holding their bits of glass against their grinding wheels. Spinoza must have been quietly gratified by his share in the great changes taking place around him. No longer would science rest on myths or fairy tales shaped by ideas that had nothing to do with reason or the actual materials of nature.

Spinoza's share in the revolution was not limited to providing tools for other people to use. Although he never achieved fame as a scientist himself, he kept himself up to date on scientific developments, and he frequently wrote about his own discoveries involving lenses, rainbows, and niter—a basic ingredient of gunpowder. But as intriguing as individual discoveries may have been in their own right, Spinoza was enthralled by something even more wondrous: the realization that there are fascinating and unexpected connections throughout the natural world.

The new science was beginning to show that matter and movement follow certain predictable patterns. The force that brings a falling apple to the ground plays a role in the planets' movements around the sun. The flow of water in a stream resembles the flow of blood in the body. A human arm and a mechanical lever work along identical principles in the lifting of weights. Only at the end of the century, after Spinoza's death, would Isaac Newton famously capture some of these amazing connections in his law of universal gravitation and his laws of motion, but individual scientists were already beginning to move in that direction. As the flurry of discoveries was beginning to reveal, beneath the endless diversity of specific cases, nature follows unchanging laws that apply in every place and every time, and those laws can be expressed in the beautifully pure language of mathematics.

Scientists of the seventeenth century, in effect, were grinding out of an unformed lump of glass a perfectly polished lens that refracted light in spectacular, orderly patterns. The seeming randomness of nature was giving way, with the application of new scientific approaches, to the splendor of systematic interconnectedness. And it was nature itself that offered up this splendor, with no need for myths or fairy tales. Nature could inspire the profound awe and devotion that some people found in their traditional worship of God.

CHAPTER FOURTEEN

THE CARTESIAN REVOLUTION

IT WAS NOT JUST RELIGIOUS OPPOSITION THAT STOOD in the way of the new science. Established patterns of thinking have an exceptionally strong hold on the human mind, and even people committed to observation and experimentation were held back by some of the old assumptions. Galileo, for example, remained committed to perfectly round planetary orbits, even though centuries of actual observation had shown obvious flaws in the idea. Scientists often failed to recognize their own allegiance to tradition, which sometimes led them to fit new evidence into the old ways of thinking. For the new science to take hold, there needed to be a far-reaching change in how people related to the traditions themselves.

This necessary change was provided by philosophy. People had always considered the old traditions to be the unquestionable starting point in the search for truth. Now people needed to take a step back and think about thinking—one of the major concerns of philosophy. There were some important questions to consider: What *is* knowledge anyway? How do we construct an accurate picture of the world? Can we *ever* be sure that we have an accurate picture of the world?

One of the most influential philosophers of the time was René Descartes, whose ideas are collectively known as Cartesian philosophy. Descartes had died in 1650, just six years before Spinoza's *cherem*, and although Descartes was French by birth, he had spent his most productive years, from 1628 to 1649, in the Dutch Republic. Once he began exploring the intellectual world beyond the Jewish community, Spinoza could hardly have avoided Descartes. Cartesian philosophy was taking Europe by storm.

Descartes began with a shocking refusal to accept on faith any ideas handed down by others. In his own search for truth, his starting point was not the old traditions but complete and utter doubt. Descartes's doubt was so sweeping that he questioned even his own existence. Although his senses seemed to provide sufficient proof that he existed, he recognized that our senses sometimes lead us to the wrong conclusions.

RENÉ DESCARTES:
In this portrait,
Descartes's rejection
of traditional ideas
is symbolized by the
placement of his foot
on a book marked with
Aristotle's name.

René Descartes,
seventeenth century.
Courtesy of the
National Gallery of Art,
Washington.

Descartes realized, however, that there was one thing about which he could be absolutely certain, and that one thing was that while he was busy doubting, he was engaged in the process of thinking. And if thinking was occurring, then the person doing the thinking—Descartes himself— had to exist. This is the meaning of Descartes's famous line *"Cogito, ergo sum"*—"I think, therefore I am." Descartes was saying, in other words, "Since I know that I am thinking, I know that I must exist." Once he had established his own existence to his satisfaction, Descartes began to investigate individual ideas step by step, admitting into his picture of the truth only those ideas that he found sufficiently convincing or, as he famously put it, "clear and distinct."

It is not difficult to see the connection between Descartes's way of arriving at the truth and the shift in how people were beginning to study nature. Descartes was arguing philosophically for the very changes that were necessary to bring science to the modern age. An accurate picture of reality, Descartes was claiming, could result only when absolutely everything was subjected to careful examination. No tradition, no matter how old and respected, should be exempt from this process.

Cartesian philosophy encouraged the shift to the new science in another major way. As he carefully constructed his picture of the truth, Descartes concluded that the body is a completely different substance from the mind—and by "mind" Descartes meant not the physical brain but the more abstract "I" that we think of as our identity. The split between the mind and the body would not be a foreign concept to anyone who has lain awake at night feeling the absolute strangeness of being attached to a particular body or to anyone who has ever been startled into asking, upon looking at a mirror, "Is that person I see there really *myself*?"

Descartes had several reasons for believing in a split between the body and the mind. For one thing, we can pretend that our bodies do not exist, but we cannot pretend that our minds do not exist— because the very act of pretending means that there is a mind to do the pretending. Furthermore, our bodies have a specific location in space, but our minds do not. And finally, a body can be physically broken into parts, but a mind cannot. Because of such differences, Descartes concluded, it is impossible to see the body and the mind as part of a single substance.

This idea may seem to be no more than an interesting philosophical curiosity, but its impact was enormous. Descartes had single-handedly dealt a death blow to the notion that physical objects behave as they do because they contain intelligent spirits or souls. Descartes did not necessarily deny the existence of such spirits or souls, but he effectively swept them off to the side. It now became possible to examine physical objects as just that— physical objects. No longer would science have to stop at the threshold of unknowable forces. Now science could analyze every aspect of the physical world and chart out the nature of physical objects as clearly and precisely as if they were machines. Myth and fairy tale would give way to universal laws of matter and motion.

If it is easy to see the relationship between Cartesian philosophy and the new science, it is also easy to see why there would be tremendous opposition to Descartes. Descartes's casting of everything into doubt and his faith in reason's power to arrive at the truth shook the intellectual and religious foundations of Europe. Descartes was essentially calling for everyone to start over, to undo entire structures of learning and knowledge and belief that had been built over centuries. And if one arrived at the truth by thinking, not by automatically accepting what others said, what would happen to religion, which was, after all, so heavily based on obedience to tradition?

Even God seemed under attack in Cartesian philosophy. Descartes himself believed in God, but the Cartesian separation between mind and body made God seem less relevant. If physical objects indeed follow predictable laws in machinelike ways, what is God's role in the universe? At best, God is the force that set the laws up in the first place but then left everything to work on its own. At worst, God is an outdated idea that needs to go the same way as the myths that were once used to explain the natural world.

It is therefore no surprise that when Spinoza first gained exposure to Descartes's ideas, conflicts over Cartesian philosophy were raging throughout Europe. Religious leaders, concerned that even the faith of simple people would not survive the Cartesian assault, were doing their best to combat the threat. Since universities were most responsible for the spread of Cartesian philosophy, they became the major battleground. The University of Leiden, not far from Amsterdam, was a prime example. The institution was the oldest and most highly regarded university in the Dutch Republic, and Descartes had himself studied mathematics there in 1630. But in both 1646 and 1647, the university's leaders issued decrees against teaching Cartesianism, and even the government of Holland got involved, issuing a similar decree for the university in 1656. These decrees pleased traditionalists but ultimately did little to stem the tide of the new intellectual movement. Several of Leiden's prominent professors ignored the rules, and the philosophy department, at least, became a stronghold of Cartesian thought.

Cartesianism fascinated Spinoza. Ever since his teenage years, he had been seeking truth in the same way that Descartes recommended. Spinoza had broken away from an entire tradition of accepted knowledge and beliefs, and now he was examining everything afresh, using his own powers of reason to determine what made sense and what did not. And so, after making sufficient headway in Latin and other preparatory studies at Van den Enden's school, Spinoza resolved to deepen his understanding of Cartesian philosophy by attending classes at the University of Leiden. There he was able to study with prominent professors and meet like-minded students. He did not complete a degree at the university, but it was not long before he was considered an expert on Cartesian philosophy in his own right.

Back in Amsterdam, Spinoza joined a group of men highly interested in Cartesianism, and together they studied Descartes's works much as the Collegiant circles studied the Bible in their Sunday meetings. But soon Spinoza's exceptional mastery of Cartesian philosophy led the other group members to think of him more as a teacher than as a fellow member. Spinoza's reputation quickly spread beyond the group itself. Even a Danish visitor to Amsterdam took note of him, although quite scornfully: "[T]here are some atheists in Amsterdam; many of them are Cartesians, among them a certain impudent atheist Jew."

Despite what the Danish visitor reported, the fact of the matter was that most members of Spinoza's Cartesian circle were not atheists. Most members of the Cartesian circle were Collegiants who believed in God and were faithful to their own open-minded understanding of Christianity. Spinoza knew many of them through his participation in their Sunday meetings. They did not agree on all religious matters, but they all shared an earnest desire to seek truth by the light of reason. And, as time went on, they shared a growing devotion to their brilliant teacher, Spinoza.

For the rest of his life, Spinoza's closest friends were members of this group from Amsterdam. It could be quite difficult to know Spinoza well because of his quiet reserve, his steady politeness, and his ever-present guardedness about what he would say to whom. But once the distance was overcome, as it was with certain members of his study group, Spinoza showed a genuine warmth and attachment.

These friends were impressive people in their own right. There was Jan Rieuwertsz, a printer and bookseller who bravely produced books that other printers rejected for fear of offending religious

THE UNIVERSITY OF LEIDEN: In this image of the university's library, bookcases house collections devoted to theology, medicine, history, math, philosophy, literature, and law. Readers stand as they consult the books, which are chained to the shelves.

Interior of the Leiden Library by Jan Cornelis Woudanus, 1610. Prints & Photographs Division, Library of Congress, LC-USZ62-46422.

and political authorities. Rieuwertsz's well-known bookshop was, for a time, the Collegiants' meeting place. There was Jarig Jellesz, a merchant whom Spinoza had known longer than any of the others and who, like Spinoza, preferred the world of thought over the world of business. Another merchant friend was the highly educated Pieter Balling, who managed, in the midst of his demanding business life, to write a book arguing for a personal, tolerant approach to religious worship. There was also Lodewijk Meyer, the director of the Amsterdam Municipal Theater, who cared much more about philosophy, literature, and the arts than he cared for religion. And there was Adriaan Koerbagh, an outspoken thinker with some very untraditional thoughts about God and the Bible. Another member of the group, Simon Joosten de Vries, was so devoted to Spinoza that he offered an annual sum to help the young philosopher live more comfortably. But Spinoza would not accept the offer. He was comfortable enough in his simple life, he explained, and the money would be a distraction from the things he cared about most.

Spinoza could not have asked for a more devoted group of friends, and in the Cartesian philosophy that drew them together, Spinoza was finding a system of thought that genuinely excited him. If the leaders of the Nation had been hoping that Spinoza would feel despair or isolation after being kicked out of the Jewish community—the kinds of feelings that had made life so intolerable for Uriel da Costa—they would have been sorely disappointed.

CHAPTER FIFTEEN

LAUNCHING
A WRITTEN
PHILOSOPHY

BUT SPINOZA, AS USUAL, WAS UNWILLING TO ACCEPT
another person's ideas uncritically. He was
fascinated by Cartesianism, but he had plenty of
ideas of his own, many of them in direct opposition
to Descartes. Spinoza was increasingly eager to
express some of his own thoughts in writing. In the
six years following his *cherem*, he produced three
different works in which he began to outline his
own philosophical system.

Spinoza's first work, the *Treatise on the
Emendation of the Intellect*, was the most
autobiographical of all his philosophical writings.
It was in this work that Spinoza explained why
he had chosen the life of a philosopher. He had
abandoned his previous way of living because his

happiness in that life was dependent on things beyond his control. He wanted instead to find the "true good," something unaffected by the ups and downs of fortune. That true good, he determined, was knowledge—specifically, knowledge of our own place in nature. Spinoza had embraced the new science's growing understanding of nature as a vast, interconnected structure, and he enthusiastically supported the notion that human beings do not stand above and beyond nature, but exist within it, as one small part of it. For Spinoza, the highest intellectual achievement was to understand our place within nature's majestic network. This understanding necessarily involved the study of many different things: the physical world in all its diversity, our own physical existence, our minds, our passions.

The word "emendation" in the title of the treatise means "changing in order to correct or improve," and the words "emendation of the intellect" suggest that Spinoza's chief concern in the treatise was to correct or improve our process of thinking. Spinoza's grand intellectual project of understanding our place in nature cannot be achieved through haphazard or shallow thinking. We know things like our birthdays because others have reported them to us, and we know that dogs bark through our simple observation of barking dogs. But these forms of knowing are not sufficient for Spinoza's project. What is necessary is knowledge of the essences of things, a knowledge far deeper than our everyday, superficial familiarity with the world around us. Mathematical understanding—being able to grasp, for example, that if two lines are parallel to a third line then they are necessarily parallel to one another—is a prime example of this kind of knowledge.

Once we have understood enough about the essences of things and grasped their relationships to one another, we have created within our minds a mental model of the universe. Through this mental model, which of course includes ourselves, we can understand our own place within the whole of nature. But this understanding is not just something that sits in our heads. A correct understanding of our place in nature necessarily affects the way we behave and feel. Most importantly, it affects the way that we experience the ups and downs of fortune. For one thing, we are less likely to be overpowered by personal tragedy when we can step back and view ourselves as just one small piece of a much larger puzzle. Once we have arrived at this understanding of ourselves within nature and modified our behaviors and feelings accordingly, we have achieved perfection.

Spinoza never completed the *Treatise on the Emendation of the Intellect*, and the unfinished manuscript was not published until after his death. But he remained committed to its basic ideas, almost all of which reappeared in his later writings. Given the way he reworked those ideas in his later writings, it seems likely that he was dissatisfied with the way his draft was turning out. Spinoza liked order—that beautiful, eternal, crystalline structure beneath the chaotic jumble of reality. The *content* of his ideas certainly expressed that order. Understanding the essences and interrelationships of things meant looking beyond the individual, short-lived details of reality in order to identify the eternal structure that lies beneath them. But the *way* Spinoza was presenting his ideas bore no relationship to his message. Spinoza was starting to imagine a new form of writing, one more suitable for his philosophical vision. He knew that that form of writing would somehow need to imitate the language of mathematics, which concerns itself not with fleeting details but with timeless truth.

Such writing would require intense thinking and effort, and Spinoza found himself frustrated by his busy life in Amsterdam. It was wonderful to have made a circle of friends who cherished and respected him, but he needed more time to be by himself. Spinoza decided to move to the country. He chose Rijnsburg, a small village near Leiden, where he lived from 1661 to 1663. Rijnsburg was ideal in

SPINOZA'S PLACES OF RESIDENCE: Spinoza spent his entire life in a tiny swath of the Dutch Republic. After leaving Amsterdam he lived in Rijnsburg, Voorburg, and The Hague. Toward the end of his life he made a trip to Utrecht.

Adobe Stock Image, modified

that it was far enough from Amsterdam to shield him from constant interruptions yet close enough for him to make the trip back to the city when he felt like doing so. In Rijnsburg, he could also enjoy easy access to the University of Leiden.

Even in the quiet village of Rijnsburg, Spinoza tried to avoid unnecessary distractions. He rented space from a local Collegiant who lived on a peaceful street outside the village center. Spinoza set up his lens-grinding workshop toward the back of the house and took a separate room for his modest living quarters, and in those two rooms he spent most of his time. He filled his days with reading, writing, and fashioning lenses.

Although Spinoza saw his lens grinding as secondary to his philosophical work, his reputation as a craftsman was growing. In just a few years, his handiwork would receive special praise from his astronomer friend Christiaan Huygens, who described Spinoza's lenses as having "an admirable polish" and as being "very excellent." There was only one problem with his new craft. As he held the glass against the grinding wheel, fine dust blew everywhere, and it was impossible not to breathe it in. He had apparently inherited breathing problems from his mother and had always coughed a lot, but now he was coughing much more than usual.

It seemed that there was a personal price to pay for enabling others to see the world more clearly. As Spinoza soon discovered, this would be just as true of his philosophizing as of his lens grinding.

CHAPTER SIXTEEN

RADICAL VIEWS OF NATURE AND GOD

IN RIJNSBURG, SPINOZA COMPLETED A SECOND treatise, one that he had actually begun to write before leaving Amsterdam. This was the *Short Treatise on God, Man, and His Well-Being*, and its title nicely sums up its main concerns. Most importantly, in the *Short Treatise* Spinoza sketched out for the first time a core idea that soon drew upon his quiet life the howling wrath and indignation of people throughout Europe. This idea was that God is the same as nature.

Spinoza was definitely not claiming that one could commune with God in the nearest oak tree. In fact, he was not really thinking about nature as a collection of stones or trees or birds or any of the usual things we call "nature" on camping trips— or what Spinoza himself called *natura naturata* (natured nature). Instead, he was thinking about what he called *natura naturans* (naturing nature)—nature as it was being revealed by the new science as a magnificent interconnected system of laws applying in all places and at all times.

Spinoza often used the term "substance" to refer to the nature that he identified with God. According to Spinoza, everything that exists in the universe is either a substance or a mode. A substance needs nothing else to exist, but a mode exists only in connection to a substance. The connection is a bit like the one between a noun and an adjective. Adjectives like "playful," "furry," and "noisy" do not have the same grammatical independence as a noun like "puppy." It is grammatically legitimate to say, "Look at the puppy" or "Look at the playful puppy," but it is not grammatically legitimate to say, "Look at the playful." In this analogy, the puppy is the substance, while the various qualities it may or may not have—being playful, furry, and noisy, or perhaps shy, smelly, and hungry—are the modes. But Spinoza goes much further than this. According to Spinoza, there is only *one* substance in the *entire* universe. Puppies, trees, rocks, and people, along with anything else that exists in the universe, are *themselves* modes of that single, all-embracing substance.

This idea is really quite staggering. The glasses resting on one's nose, the trees shading a window, the car parked on the street, the young woman walking by on the sidewalk, the sun shining in the sky above—all of it is really just a mutation of that one basic substance into some of its various modes. That substance just happens to be glasseslike on one's nose, carlike in the street, and sunlike in the sky. Everything that exists, has ever existed, or will ever exist is part of that substance, and there is absolutely nothing beyond it. It is this infinite, single substance that Spinoza means when he speaks of nature, and this is the nature that Spinoza says is identical to God.

At first glance, this idea might not seem especially controversial. After all, if God is identical to the single substance that is nature, God is by definition eternal, infinite, and fully engaged in the world—seemingly the same God envisioned by the Judeo-Christian tradition. But nothing could be further from the truth. The identification of God with nature was a complete bombshell. Spinoza's God is reality itself, and there is absolutely nothing beyond that reality. This means that God is not transcendent—God is not a power that exists in a heaven or in any other separate and lofty domain above and beyond anything we can know or experience. This means as well that there is no creator, and there is no outside force overseeing or directing what happens in the world.

In fact, according to Spinoza, religions are mostly incorrect when they speak of God. It is meaningless to describe God as "all-knowing," "merciful," "wise," or "good" or to imagine that God is personally involved in our lives. God shows us no special favors and expects nothing from us—no sacrifices, no prayers, no specific beliefs, no ceremonies, no obedience to a particular set of rules. God has no grand plans for the world or for the human beings within it. All of these views present God anthropomorphically, as a kind of superman.

As Spinoza saw it, people fall into the trap of anthropomorphism because, as humans, they naturally conceive of perfection in entirely human terms. Many years later, Spinoza illustrated this failing with pointed humor: "I believe that a triangle, if it could speak, would likewise say that God is eminently triangular, and a circle that God's nature is eminently circular." The origins of this mistake are understandable, but the mistake is still a mistake. Again, as Spinoza later wrote, "[T]o ascribe to God those attributes which make a man perfect would be as wrong as to ascribe to a man the attributes that make perfect an elephant or an ass." God, like nature, simply *is*.

Spinoza's view of God has obvious consequences for how people should conduct their lives. If God expects nothing of us, then adhering to specific

beliefs or practicing specific rituals becomes
meaningless. If God is indifferent to human
behavior, then there is no reason to fear divine
punishment or to hope for divine reward, whether in
this life or in an imagined afterlife. With Spinoza's
view of God, much of what we associate with
traditional religion simply falls away.

The *Short Treatise on God, Man, and His Well-
Being* was really an expansion of the *Treatise on
the Emendation of the Intellect*. In his first treatise,
Spinoza had formulated the idea that people reach
perfection by understanding their place in nature.
Now, in his second treatise, he explained what this
project involves. For one thing, understanding our
place in nature means recognizing that there is no
outside, godlike force to interfere with the eternal
and universal laws of nature. This means that
absolutely everything in the world is the result of
long chains of cause and effect. Nothing could be
other than it is because everything that happens
does so necessarily.

Most shockingly, since there is absolutely
nothing beyond nature, the necessity of all things
includes human activity. Our sense of our own
freedom, in other words, is a sheer illusion. We
believe that we are free to act as we please only
because we are unaware of the long chains of cause
and effect that lead us to a particular thought or

action. Later in his life, Spinoza clarified this idea for a friend by asking him to picture a stone that has been flung through the air. "Furthermore conceive, if you please," Spinoza added, "that while continuing in motion the stone thinks, and knows that it is endeavoring, as far as in it lies, to continue in motion. Now this stone, since it is conscious only of its endeavor and is not at all indifferent, will surely think it is completely free, and that it continues in motion for no other reason than that it so wishes." All of us, according to Spinoza, are stones flung through the air. Because we are unaware of the ways in which our desires and actions have been determined, we mistakenly believe that we desire and act freely.

Throughout his life, Spinoza confronted the counterargument that if people have no freedom, society would not be able to insist on moral behavior. If a person cannot control the chains of cause and effect that lead to particular thoughts or behaviors, how can that person be held responsible for what he or she does? Spinoza was not bothered by the question because he firmly maintained that freedom or lack of freedom does not change the desirability of good behavior. Or, as he later expressed the point in relation to bad behavior, "Wicked men are no less to be feared and no less dangerous when they are necessarily wicked." For Spinoza, the idea that we have no freedom does just the opposite of what so many people feared: instead of discouraging good behavior, it enables us to engage in the best behavior possible. Once we recognize that everything happens necessarily, we can set aside our destructive habits and passions. We no longer need to spend our time and energy on our hopes or our fears, and we can relax in our contemplation of the unchanging reality that is God, or nature. That contemplation is not a religious experience in the usual sense, but an engagement in philosophy and science to reveal the immutable laws that govern all of existence, linking everything together in chains of necessity.

The necessity of all things and the rejection of human freedom are not the only radical ideas connected to the identification of God with nature. Another claim that Spinoza made is just as staggering. This claim is that there is no genuine reality to the categories of good and evil. If God just *is*, just as nature just *is*, there is no higher authority to tell us what is good and what is evil. It makes no sense to applaud or to condemn a lion that attacks a harmless gazelle. That lion is simply doing what lions do. Good and evil, in other words, are not parts of the essences of things but are ideas that we concoct in our minds. The terms "good" and "evil" do no more than describe relative or comparative connections. We say, for instance, that a person is bad only in relation to other people who are better, and we say that an apple is good only in relation to other apples that are worse—and we generally make those judgments based on how personally useful we find things to be. There is no absolute good or absolute evil.

Spinoza's ideas could hardly have clashed more starkly with the religious culture of seventeenth-century Europe. Western religions based on the Judeo-Christian heritage insist on a God who is above and beyond our experience, a God who created the universe and continues to sustain it. But Spinoza denied that God is in any way transcendent. Western religions trust that the all-knowing, all-powerful, and perfectly good God cares for us and gets actively involved in our lives. But Spinoza denied that God does anything more than exist in a completely impersonal way. Western religions believe that God unrestrictedly manipulates all things according to a grand plan with a reason or purpose for everything. But Spinoza denied God any freedom to make things other than they are. Western religions assume that people occupy a unique place in nature and exercise free will. But Spinoza denied that people are any less bound by cause and effect than any other part of nature. Western religions maintain that good and evil are real and absolute values defined by a God who demands appropriate behavior. But Spinoza saw good and evil as entirely human constructs.

It is not surprising that, with views such as these, Spinoza was readily labeled an atheist. But Spinoza always found that label perplexing. Years later, he asserted that only a complete unfamiliarity with his lifestyle could lead anyone to charge him with atheism. With his era's typical assumption that only bad people deny God's existence, he wrote, "[A]theists are usually inordinately fond of honours and riches, which I have always despised, as is known to all who are acquainted with me." Furthermore, Spinoza pointed out that he was always talking about God—insisting, in fact, that a person's supreme happiness consists in loving God—and that this was certainly not the kind of language that an atheist would use.

Of course, given what Spinoza really meant when he talked about God, it is perhaps unfair to fault the public for considering him an atheist. When he used the word "God" in the *Short Treatise*, he meant the all-embracing nature of which we are just one small part, and when he talked about "loving God," he meant the intellectual contemplation of nature that should be our goal. He used the title "That God Is a Cause of All Things" for a chapter explaining that nothing exists beyond the single substance that is God or nature, and he used the term "divine predestination" for his claim that nothing in nature could possibly be other than it is. Spinoza employed religious language to present ideas entirely at odds with traditional religions.

Once Spinoza's writings became well-known—and notorious—he was often accused of cynical scheming. He was using religious terminology, it was said, as a sneaky trick to further his goal of corrupting people and winning them over to his evil atheism. But Spinoza was an honest man. He did not always tell people what he was thinking, but when he did choose to speak his mind, he did so directly, without deception. It has more recently—and more generously—been said that Spinoza used religious terminology as a kind of code, a language that would present his ideas clearly only to those who sympathized with his views. The code would have protected Spinoza from those who strongly disagreed with him and shielded less sophisticated thinkers from ideas to which even Spinoza believed they ought not to be exposed. But it is hard to believe that anyone but the most careless reader would be fooled by such a code. It takes very little scratching beneath the surface to see what Spinoza really means.

Perhaps the key to Spinoza's motivation comes from his most poignant use of a religious term. This is his use of the word "blessedness," by which he meant the perfection we achieve when we understand our own place within nature. Spinoza had abandoned the religion of his youth and was not particularly attracted to any of the other religious options to which he had been exposed since. Nonetheless, the man whose name meant "blessed" in three languages was still very much on a quest for blessedness, absolutely determined to achieve a state higher and better than the one we usually occupy. Although Spinoza set out to do this without belief in a traditional God, religious language must have been, for him, the natural way to express the glory of his vision. Spinoza, in many ways, was a passionately religious man without a religion.

CHAPTER SEVENTEEN

CAUTION AND CARTESIAN LESSONS

SPINOZA WAS OF COURSE AWARE THAT HE WAS expressing some very dangerous ideas in the *Short Treatise*. Outrage from the Calvinists was to be expected, but even generally liberal-minded Christians were likely to take offense. And so Spinoza, at least for now, did not want the *Short Treatise* to be widely distributed. In fact, he had written it specifically for the members of his Cartesian group back in Amsterdam. Spinoza's friends had long realized that their teacher's brilliance went far beyond his ability to explain Descartes, and they had been earnestly pressing him to lay out his own philosophy in writing. Their requests intensified once Spinoza moved away from Amsterdam and was not readily available to explain his ideas in person. The plan was for the group to study the *Short Treatise* in Spinoza's absence and contact him by letter with their questions or doubts. Every so often Spinoza would make his way to Amsterdam, where he would be able to meet with the group face to face.

But even the very limited distribution of the *Short Treatise* to a highly select group of people could prove problematic. Spinoza's friends were obviously quite liberal thinkers, but Spinoza's ideas were likely to shock even them. And so Spinoza included a direct message to his friends at the end of the *Short Treatise*: "So, to make an end of all this, it only remains for me still to say to my friends to whom I write this: Be not astonished at these novelties; for it is very well known to you that a thing does not therefore cease to be true because it is not accepted by many." Spinoza ended with a plea for caution: "And also, as the character of the age in which we live is not unknown to you, I would beg of you most earnestly to be very careful about the communication of these things to others."

Spinoza's message to his friends at the end of the *Short Treatise* showed his characteristic combination of fearlessness and caution. Spinoza boldly pursued his ideas as far as they would take him, but he was also wary about how other people might react. Since he wanted little more than peace and quiet to think for himself, he knew that he would have to exercise great care in making his views public.

In fact, Spinoza felt so strongly about the need for caution that it became his motto. He designed a seal for himself containing the word *caute*, the Latin word for caution. Over the word was the image of a rose whose thorns (*espinos* in Spanish) hinted at his name. Around the image he placed the letters *B*, *D*, and *S*, for Benedict de Spinoza. He had this design inscribed on the signet ring that he used as a stamp on his personal letters. In this way both he and his friends had a constant reminder of the warning that appeared at the end of the *Short Treatise*. The forces of intolerance were everywhere, and Spinoza had every intention of avoiding them so that he could be left alone to do his work.

Caute meant that Spinoza often held back his true views from the people with whom he interacted. Soon after he moved to Rijnsburg, he had a very welcome visit from a man named Henry Oldenburg. Oldenburg lived in London, but he frequently traveled to continental Europe in his work for the Royal Society, an organization that still exists today to promote scientific education and research. Back in Spinoza's day, the Royal Society was a brand-new organization founded specifically to support the new science based on observation and experimentation. The Society's commitment to the new science was nicely summed up by the motto its founders chose, the Latin phrase *Nullius in verba*, translating roughly into "Take nobody's word for it." As part of his work for the Society, Oldenburg visited different countries. His goals were to stay informed about the most recent scientific developments and to establish international communication among like-minded scholars and scientists.

On a visit to the Dutch Republic, Oldenburg heard repeatedly of a brilliant Cartesian scholar in Rijnsburg and determined that his trip would be incomplete without meeting such a remarkable individual. Spinoza, not yet thirty years old, must have felt keenly gratified to be singled out by such a distinguished scholar. And, of course, Spinoza could not have been more enthusiastic about Oldenburg's work. The two men enjoyed their face-to-face discussion so much that they began writing to each other about philosophy, optics, chemistry, and other shared interests. Their lively correspondence continued for most of their lives.

But even with this man, *caute* remained Spinoza's approach. During their meeting in Rijnsburg, Spinoza skillfully steered their conversation clear of his radical views about nature and God. Oldenburg did not know just what Spinoza was avoiding, but he definitely sensed Spinoza's restraint. In the first letter he wrote to Spinoza after returning to London, Oldenburg urged his new friend to share his views more readily. "[W]e then spoke about such

SPINOZA'S SEAL: A thorny rose alluding to
Spinoza's name is surrounded by his initials as well as
his motto, "caute."

Letter to Leibniz (Letter 46), November 9, 1671. Gottfried Wilhelm
Leibniz Bibliothek, Hanover.

Reproduction of seal from Leben Benedikt's *Von Spinos*a by Moses
Philipson (Braunschweig: Verlag der Schulbuchhandlung, 1790).
HathiTrust Digital Library.

important topics as through a lattice-window and only in a cursory way, and in the meantime all these things continue to torment me," he complained. But *caute* remained Spinoza's watchword, and the lattice remained in place throughout their many years of correspondence. It took fourteen years after their meeting in Rijnsburg, after he read the book that made Spinoza an infamous household name throughout Europe, for Oldenburg—completely horrified—to grasp the full extent of the philosopher's views.

Another example of *caute* concerns Johannes Casearius, a University of Leiden student who sought out Spinoza for private instruction in Cartesian philosophy. In his zeal to pursue these lessons, matched only by his unconcern at being an imposition, Casearius rented lodgings in the same house where Spinoza was living. If this had not been irritating enough, Casearius turned out to be intellectually immature, certainly not yet ready for Spinoza's true opinions. "Indeed, there is no one who is more of a trouble to me, and no one with whom I have had to be more on my guard," Spinoza wrote to his Amsterdam friend Simon Joosten de Vries, who was terribly jealous of Casearius's opportunity to learn from Spinoza at all hours of the day. "So I should like you and all our acquaintances," Spinoza continued, "not to communicate my opinions to him until he will have reached a more mature age."

There was, however, one very positive outcome of Spinoza's lessons with Casearius. To present Descartes's philosophy to his less-than-brilliant student, Spinoza began experimenting with the kind of orderly, methodical presentation he had been imagining for his own work, the form of writing that would imitate mathematics in its ability to convey the timeless truth beneath the messy surface of reality.

Spinoza hit upon the geometric proof as an especially suitable model for presenting Cartesian philosophy. In the geometric proof, one begins with a small number of basic definitions (such as "a point is a specific, dimensionless location in space") and a small number of basic truths (such as "if A = B and B = C, then A = C"). From those starting points, one is able to construct ever more complicated mathematical statements (such as "triangle DEF is congruent to triangle XYZ"), each new statement emerging only from what has already been established as true. In other words, the geometric proof does for math precisely what Descartes was doing for his picture of the truth. Descartes started off with a small number of very basic ideas that he had determined were clearly and distinctly true.

Then he used those basic truths to arrive logically at ever more complex conclusions.

In his lessons to Casearius, Spinoza eagerly began rearranging Descartes's ideas in the style of the geometric proof. The results were gratifying. There was beauty in the perfect match between the ideas and their format, and there was pleasure in stripping down Descartes's vision to its bare essentials so that its eternal, underlying structure could be more easily grasped. But even more than beauty or pleasure, there was truth. Mathematics was the way to certainty. Its assumptions and methods were clear for all to see, its arguments were logical and systematic, and its conclusions were beyond dispute. Mathematics had begun to demonstrate the unquestionable truths of the new science. Spinoza was now harnessing mathematics to do the same for philosophy.

Spinoza did not actually write down his geometric presentation of Descartes's ideas, at least not at first. It was Casearius who dutifully recorded them in writing as Spinoza dictated them orally. But soon the members of the Cartesian circle back in Amsterdam, ever jealous of Casearius, were requesting their own copy. And when they saw what Spinoza had produced, they realized that they had a masterwork in their hands. Spinoza's guide to Descartes was unsurpassed, and they predicted that it would become the standard textbook for anyone interested in Cartesian philosophy. They urged Spinoza to publish his lessons for the general public and enthusiastically extended their help. Lodewijk Meyer offered to serve as Spinoza's editor, and Jan Rieuwertsz offered his assistance as printer and bookseller.

The idea of publishing this work was troubling to Spinoza. He was far from agreeing with everything in Cartesian philosophy, and he did not want people to assume that his own views were the same as Descartes's. One of the major differences between the two philosophers concerned the number of substances in the world. Since Spinoza believed that the universe consists of a single, infinite, and eternal substance, he rejected Descartes's division between body and mind.

This basic disagreement between the philosophies of the two thinkers had important consequences. Because Descartes viewed mind and body as two distinct things, he could claim that different rules applied to each. Physical bodies might have to follow certain universal laws such as the laws of motion or gravity, but the human mind, composed of an entirely different substance, was another story altogether. Descartes, in effect, had found a way to maintain traditional beliefs at the same time that he supported the new science.

Because of the special nature of their minds, human beings could still exercise free will and their souls could still enjoy immortality. In the meantime, their bodies, along with the rest of the physical world, could be studied as if they were simply machines.

Spinoza entirely rejected this line of reasoning. If the mind and body are two separate substances, how do they interact at all? We know that they must interact in some way—otherwise, how could we ever throw a ball or pull a wagon or put pen to paper? Spinoza argued instead that the mind and the body are part of a single substance—the only substance. With this philosophical step, he swept away traditional views of human significance and worth. The human mind is just as much a machine as anything else in nature. Human beings have no special status, free will is an illusion, and there is no personal soul to survive the death of the body. Spinoza was not afraid of such unnerving ideas. Only by facing them squarely and bravely, he felt, can we establish a new, more rational foundation for human worth and happiness.

Spinoza agreed to publish his lessons on Descartes only if the volume presented his own opinions as well. The result was *Parts I and II of René Descartes's The Principles of Philosophy, demonstrated in the geometric manner* by Benedict de Spinoza of Amsterdam, along with an appendix,

RENATI DES CARTES

PRINCIPIORUM
PHILOSOPHIÆ

Pars I, & II,

More Geometrico demonstratæ

PER

BENEDICTUM de SPINOZA *Amstelodamensem.*

Accesserunt Ejusdem

COGITATA METAPHYSICA,

In quibus difficiliores , quæ tam in parte Metaphysices generali , quàm speciali occurrunt , quæstiones breviter explicantur.

AMSTELODAMI,

Apud JOHANNEM RIEWERTS, *in vico vulgò dicto*, de Dirk van Assen-steeg, *sub signo Martyrologii.* 1663.

DESCARTES'S PRINCIPLES OF PHILOSOPHY AND METAPHYSICAL THOUGHTS: This title page identifies Spinoza as the author, Jan Rieuwertsz as the publisher, and Amsterdam as the place of publication. This is the only one of Spinoza's published works to offer such forthright information either during or immediately after his lifetime.

Title page of *Renati Des Cartes Principiorum philosophiæ pars I, & II, more geometrico demonstratæ per Benedictum de Spinoza . . .* 1663. Rare Book and Manuscript Library, Columbia University in the City of New York.

the *Metaphysical Thoughts*. The first part of the book faithfully presented Descartes's ideas, while the second part gave a glimpse of Spinoza's own views about God, necessity, and free will.

Spinoza hoped that the double volume, and particularly its second part, would pave the way for people to consider the more fully developed views that he had been cautiously sharing with only his closest friends. More and more he was feeling the urgency of sharing his ideas with a broader audience. It was not a question of fame or money, which meant nothing to him, but an eager desire, as he wrote to his friend Lodewijk Meyer, to work for "the benefit of all men" and "to spread the truth."

As Spinoza's friends had predicted, the Cartesian lessons were a huge success. The original Latin version of the book was so highly acclaimed that Spinoza and his friends decided to issue a Dutch version. Pieter Balling, one of the study group's members, gladly undertook the translation into Dutch, which made the work available to a much larger readership within the Republic. Spinoza's reputation as a leading Cartesian was firmly established, and he seemed well poised to shift the spotlight to his own philosophical system.

CHAPTER EIGHTEEN

PLAGUES OF BODY
AND MIND

DURING THE SPRING OF 1663, IN THE THICK OF HIS
work on *Descartes's Principles of Philosophy* and the
Metaphysical Thoughts, Spinoza was arranging
a move to the village of Voorburg. He was still
aiming for solitude without too much isolation:
Voorburg was just two miles from The Hague, the
seat of Holland's provincial government and of the
Dutch Republic's national government. Spinoza's
new setting would provide the peace of a village
alongside the intellectual life of a city.

Spinoza rented lodgings in the home of Daniel
Tydeman, a man he had probably met through
mutual Collegiant contacts. Tydeman was an artist
who was happy to give Spinoza some lessons in
drawing, and Spinoza showed some talent for his
new hobby. He especially enjoyed sketching ink and
charcoal portraits of the people who came to visit

him, and he also tried his hand at self-portraiture. In one flight of fancy, he drew his own face on the body of a fisherman bearing a net over his shoulder.

But life turned somber just a few months after Spinoza's move to Voorburg. During the summer of 1663, bubonic plague broke out in northern Europe. The plague, fortunately quite rare nowadays, is a bacterial infection spread primarily by small rodents and their fleas, and it is highly contagious. The infection triggers painful swelling in the lymph glands and causes the death of body tissue, especially in the fingers, toes, nose, and lips. Because this dead tissue turns black, the plague became known during the Middle Ages as the "Black Death." Unless it is treated, the plague kills about two-thirds of its victims within just four days.

In 1663, the only defense against the plague was avoiding it. Cities were the most dangerous places because of their high concentrations of people, rodents, and filth, and anyone who could flee to the country did so. Voorburg was a small town, but the nearness of The Hague made it risky to remain there. Spinoza gladly accepted the invitation of Simon Joosten de Vries to stay at a family farm for much of the winter of 1663–1664. It was not an especially happy time. The previous June, De Vries had lost his mother, his brother, and his sister-in-law to the dread disease. Soon bad news arrived from

Amsterdam. Pieter Balling's young son had also succumbed.

For Spinoza, philosophy was a way of life, not just an academic subject. His reaction to his friends' tragedies was entirely in keeping with his view that we are simply part of nature, with its long, interconnected chains of cause and effect that determine everything. Writing to console Balling over his recent loss, Spinoza remarked, "It caused me no little sorrow and anxiety, though that has much diminished when I reflect on the good sense and strength of character which enable you to scorn the adversities of fortune, or what is thought of as such, at the very time when they are assailing you with their strongest weapons." A right-minded person, one who understands that the blows of fortune are simply part of the necessity of nature, does not allow tragedy to become personally overwhelming.

There was comfort, at least, in the extended time that Spinoza and De Vries could spend together. Philosophy had become Spinoza's main connection to others. When he was not busy working in solitude, he was happiest when he could discuss his ideas with like-minded people. "For my part, of all things that are not under my control," he wrote in one of his letters, "what I most value is to enter into a bond of friendship with sincere lovers of truth. For

I believe that such a loving relationship affords us a serenity surpassing any other boon in the whole wide world."

Because of his eagerness for philosophical companionship, Spinoza occasionally forgot his usual caution. The letter in which Spinoza described his delight over friendship with sincere lovers of truth was itself an attempt to establish such a relationship—but with someone who turned out to be entirely the wrong sort of person. During his stay with De Vries at the farm, Spinoza received a communication from Willem van Blijenbergh, a grain merchant with philosophical aspirations. Blijenbergh expressed a great deal of enthusiasm over *Descartes's Principles of Philosophy* and the *Metaphysical Thoughts*, which he had recently read. But he wanted clarification on some points that had confused him. Based on Blijenbergh's letter, Spinoza was quick to embrace him as a fellow spirit:

> *I gathered . . . that you are deeply devoted to truth, which you make the sole aim of all your endeavors. Since I have exactly the same objective, this has determined me not only to grant without stint your request to answer to the best of my ability the questions which you are now sending me and will send in the future, but*

also to do everything in my power conducive to further acquaintance and sincere friendship.

Spinoza readily spelled out for Blijenbergh some of the radical ideas at which he had only hinted in the *Metaphysical Thoughts.* He explained, for instance, that God neither demands nor expects anything from people and that good and evil are not objective realities. He also presented his view that the Bible is not the ultimate source of truth about the world. Spinoza had never revealed his ideas quite so fully to anyone outside his inner circle.

Had he known just the title of a book that Blijenbergh had recently written, Spinoza would have been far less enthusiastic. The lengthy title ran as follows: *The knowledge of God and Religion, defended against the Outrages of Atheists, In which it is demonstrated with clear and natural reasons that God has created and revealed a Religion, that God also wishes to be served in accordance with this religion, and that the Christian Religion corresponds not only to the Religion revealed by God but also to our innate reason.* Spinoza, of course, thoroughly rejected the anthropomorphic view of God. He would never have agreed with Blijenbergh that God "created and revealed a Religion" or that God "wishes to be served" in any way whatsoever.

It obviously took very little time for the huge difference between the two men to become apparent. At the very beginning of his second letter, Blijenbergh explained that when his own use of reason led him to conclusions that seemed to contradict the Bible, he always deferred to the Bible—"And little wonder, since I wish to continue steadfast in the belief that that Word is the Word of God, that is, that it has proceeded from the highest and most perfect God who possesses far more perfection than I can conceive." With such a starting point, it is no surprise that Blijenbergh found many of Spinoza's ideas utterly unacceptable.

As soon as Spinoza recognized the vast gulf between himself and his correspondent, he politely but firmly suggested that they end their relationship: "I see that we disagree not only in the conclusions to be drawn by a chain of reasoning from first principles, but in those very same first principles, so that I hardly believe that our correspondence can be for our mutual instruction." But Blijenbergh was a persistent man, and it took a year and a half of letter writing, along with a meeting in person, before Spinoza could rid himself of the unwanted association.

As his overhasty embrace of Blijenbergh demonstrates, alongside Spinoza's street-savvy caution ran a naïve faith in the community of reason. He was keen to believe that other people shared his honest pursuit of the truth, and once he became convinced of this, he could not resist the compulsion to share his ideas. And since he saw in his own ideas the absolute, unquestionable truth, he took it for granted that any reasonable person would be entirely convinced by what he had to say. This was the same tendency that had led Spinoza, many years earlier, to reveal his true thoughts to the Nation's spies. He had thought that he was engaging in a sincere philosophical discussion with genuinely interested people, but he was really just providing them with the abundant evidence of heresy that promptly led to his *cherem*.

This same naïve tendency was at work in Spinoza's grand hopes for spreading his own system of thought. As it turned out, Blijenbergh's horrified reactions were a fairly accurate preview of the public reception Spinoza could expect for his ideas. Spinoza was far too buoyant in his hopes that *Descartes's Principles of Philosophy* and the *Metaphysical Thoughts* would establish his reputation firmly enough for people to consider and accept his own philosophy. That double volume was the only writing that Spinoza dared to publish under his own name during his lifetime.

CHAPTER NINETEEN

POLITICAL
UPHEAVALS
AND THE ETHICS

BY 1665, THE PLAGUE HAD ALREADY CLAIMED THE
lives of 34,000 people in Amsterdam alone—more
than ten percent of the city's population. Although
the terrible epidemic would ravage the Dutch
Republic for at least another year, the worst of it
was over. But the year 1665 brought a new set of
troubles.

On the national level, there was the outbreak of
war with England, with whom the Dutch Republic
had long competed over sea routes and control of
international trade. In 1664, hostilities between the
two countries had resulted in the Dutch surrender
of New Amsterdam, which the English promptly
renamed New York. The ill will deepened when
the English king, Charles II, tried to install as the

Republic's head of state his own nephew, William III. William III was in fact a member of the Dutch royal house and the rightful heir to the position of stadtholder, which was essentially the position of king. But the monarchy had fallen out of favor as the merchant oligarchy gained political power, and when William's father died in 1650, the position was dropped. For a decade and a half, William had been waiting in the wings to be restored to power, and now he was enjoying the support of the English.

In trying to restore William III as stadtholder, Charles II was mainly looking after his own welfare. The king expected William's gratitude for English backing to express itself in policies favorable to England. Furthermore, Charles anticipated benefits from William's inevitable impact on the merchant-Calvinist balance. William would naturally oppose the merchants who had eliminated the position of stadtholder, and by doing so, he would enjoy the support of the Calvinists, who were already predisposed to favor him. The Calvinists felt that a single ruler would be most effective in establishing uniform religious standards throughout the country, and they understood the Bible to show a marked preference for monarchy. Any strengthening of the Calvinists meant a weakening of the merchants, and the weakening of the merchants would benefit England's own commercial interests. Charles II, in other words, planned to use William III to sway the Republic's internal tensions in England's favor.

For now, however, the merchants remained in power, and the government's opposition to England was fierce. A full-blown Anglo-Dutch war was officially declared in March 1665. The Dutch suffered a devastating string of losses but finally turned the tables in 1666. Defeated and demoralized—and by then suffering horrifically from its own outbreak of the plague—England signed a peace treaty in July 1667. The treaty allowed England to keep New York, but other captured colonies had to be returned to the Dutch.

Most of the battles took place at sea, and Spinoza, neither a soldier nor a sailor, found his personal life largely unchanged. But he characteristically found in the war an occasion for philosophical reflection. "For my part," he wrote in a letter to Oldenburg, "these troubles move me neither to laughter nor again to tears, but rather to philosophising, and to a closer observation of human nature. For I do not think it right to laugh at nature, and far less to grieve over it, reflecting that men, like all else, are only a part of nature." Even human folly and cruelty, for Spinoza, were part of the entirety of nature. For his own part, the philosopher just wanted his usual peace and quiet. "I let everyone go his own way," he told Oldenburg. "Those who wish can by all means die for their own good, as long as I am allowed to live for truth."

The year 1665 brought challenges on the local level as well. The village of Voorburg was in the middle of a prickly disagreement over who would be the next pastor of the local church. One group in the town favored a strict Calvinist leader, while another group, including Spinoza's landlord, Daniel Tydeman, favored a more liberal candidate. Spinoza was not a Christian and not directly concerned in the dispute, but the Calvinist sympathizers seized on the connection between Spinoza and Tydeman as a way to damage Tydeman's reputation and discredit his entire side in the controversy. Despite Spinoza's quiet and cautious ways, it was now clear that negative rumors about him were spreading in an alarming fashion. Those around him were guilty by association.

Spinoza's health was also worsening. His breathing troubles had become more acute, and he was suffering from a stubborn fever. Following the common practice of his day, he took medicine made of red roses to ease his breathing, and he bled himself to reduce his fever. He soon felt better, but the relief meant only that his symptoms had temporarily faded, not that the underlying ailment had gone away. He would never be genuinely free of the medical condition that eventually claimed his life.

But Spinoza was not one to give up. In the midst of all the turbulence on national, local, and personal levels, he was working on his ambitious plan to articulate his complete philosophical system in writing. The recent success of his geometric presentation of Cartesianism convinced him that the same format would work for his own system of thought.

If anything, his own ideas called even more urgently than Cartesianism for a geometric presentation. Aside from his step-by-step approach to constructing a picture of the truth, an approach that he shared with Descartes, Spinoza's particular view of nature resembled the geometric proof. If nature consisted of long chains of cause and effect that determined absolutely everything, nature could be aptly paralleled by the chains of reasoning that form a geometric proof. In both cases, the connection between a specific element and the next one in the sequence would be completely logical and utterly inescapable.

Another feature of Spinoza's philosophy that cried out for a geometric presentation was his appeal to step back and see the world from a larger perspective, the perspective that enables us to see that we are simply one small part of nature.

Spinoza termed this larger perspective *sub specie aeternitatis* (under the aspect of eternity) because it necessarily moves us beyond the trivial particulars of our lives and enables us to see beyond the usual considerations of time and place. The impersonal and eternal character of this perspective is fittingly echoed by the impersonal and eternal character of the geometric proof. Spinoza's philosophy, like mathematics, ignores the particular as it exalts the universal.

Finally, there was Spinoza's strong sense of mission. Philosophy, for Spinoza, could never be just a collection of interesting thoughts to intrigue a select group of people until a new set of ideas comes along. Spinoza wanted to do nothing less than save the world. If he were to succeed in this lofty goal, he would have to do a superb job of convincing people that his ideas were unquestionably right. The geometric format would show in a logically systematic way why his conclusions were beyond dispute.

It was because of Spinoza's sense of mission that he chose *Ethics* as the title of his work. The word "ethics" refers to a body of principles about right and wrong that is intended as a guide to appropriate behavior. At first glance, however, much of the *Ethics* seems to have little to do with ethical concerns. In the first section of the work, for instance, Spinoza explains at length his ideas about substance, that infinite and eternal entity that Spinoza has in mind when he talks about God or nature. The characteristics of substance seem largely irrelevant to how people should behave. But what Spinoza is really doing is building up, in a very methodical way, a new understanding of the universe that will necessarily affect the way in which people conduct their lives.

The *Ethics* is divided into five parts. The first two parts, which focus on the nature of substance, elaborate on many of the ideas that Spinoza had already presented to his circle of friends in the *Short Treatise*. All of nature consists of a single substance, and that substance is identical to God. There is absolutely nothing beyond substance, which is nature, which is God, and it is therefore meaningless to think about God as an outside force acting freely upon the world or as a kind of superpower with human qualities. There is absolutely no freedom for maneuvering of any sort in nature. Everything in the world is exactly the way it is because it could not possibly be otherwise, "just as from the nature of a triangle it follows from eternity and to eternity that its three angles are equal to two right angles." In a brief review of these ideas later in the book, Spinoza uses a phrase that has become a famous encapsulation of his position:

"Deus, sive natura," meaning "God, or nature"—a statement so provocative that after Spinoza's death, his friends removed it from the Dutch translation for fear of its reaching too broad an audience.

Spinoza insists that this God, or nature, is the only substance that exists; even the apparently profound difference between mind and body need not lead us to the conclusion that there is more than one substance. To explain how two such different things are really part of one substance, Spinoza introduces the idea that substance has essential characteristics—what he calls "attributes"— through which it is known. One of these attributes is extension, the physical taking up of space, and another one is thought. Everything we encounter in the universe is an expression, or mode, of these two attributes. Physical bodies are modes of extension, and ideas are modes of thought.

Extension and thought are not two different things but two different ways of looking at exactly the same thing. As Spinoza puts it, "The order and connection of ideas is the same as the order and connection of things." For example, "a circle existing in Nature and the idea of the existing circle . . . are one and the same thing, explicated through different attributes." In other words, ideas are related to one another in the same way that their corresponding physical bodies are related to one another. If the

wind causes an apple to fall from a tree, the idea of
that wind bears the same causal relationship to the
idea of that apple.

Extension and thought operate in the same
way for human beings, who are a part of nature
like anything else. Viewed through the attribute of
extension, a person is a body, and viewed through
the attribute of thought, a person is a mind. Because
these are just two different ways of viewing precisely
the same substance, there is none of Descartes's
split between the body and the mind. And since the
mind is just as bound by the cause-and-effect chains
of nature as any physical, extended object, it can be
studied just as if it were a machine. There is no such
thing as human freedom.

Spinoza expands upon this lack of freedom in
the third and fourth parts of the *Ethics*, in which
he details how human emotions, like everything
else about us, follow the laws of nature. As
Spinoza describes his project, "I shall consider
human actions and appetites just as if it were an
investigation into lines, planes, or bodies." Although
anything we do results from necessary chains of
cause and effect, Spinoza draws a clear distinction
between what he calls actions and what he calls
passions. Actions are generated by the necessity of
our own nature, whereas passions are generated by
the necessity of things outside us. If I help another

person because of my internal sense of justice, I am engaging in an action. I have relied on my use of reason and my grasp of truth, and I act with a self-sufficiency that gives me a healthy, expansive sense of myself. If, however, I help another person because I want to win accolades from observers, I am engaging in a passion. I have placed my happiness in the hands of other people, an element that I cannot control, and my sense of well-being suffers. All of us are caught up in passions whenever we depend on things that may or may not work out the way we hope—the fate of our investments in an uncertain market, the response of someone with whom we have fallen in love, the number of followers we have garnered on social media. Spinoza's title for Part IV of the *Ethics* nicely sums up his view of such a life: "Of Human Bondage, or the Strength of the Emotions."

Escape from this bondage is Spinoza's concern in the fifth and final part of the *Ethics*. We can never entirely eliminate our passions, we can never have any real control over our circumstances, and we cannot even control the chains of cause and effect that make our minds work in a particular way. What is within our power, however, is the ability to engage in self-reliant actions, not externally generated passions—in other words, to reduce the impact of outside forces upon our lives. The ultimate action is to pursue the highest form of knowledge and to grasp things *sub specie aeternitatis*. Once again, the title of the section is revealing: "Of the Power of the Intellect, or Human Freedom." It is only when we exercise the power of our intellects that we are free.

Spinoza had written about many of these ideas before, but the *Ethics* was more systematic, complete, and ambitious than anything he had yet produced. It was also the first comprehensive statement of his philosophy that he was addressing not just to his tight circle of friends but to the larger public. Spinoza still needed to clarify and refine the text, but he was finally realizing the project that he had been dreaming about for years. His aim was nothing short of leading the world from the oppression of slavery to the blessedness of freedom.

CHAPTER TWENTY

SURGES OF RELIGIOUS
UNREASON

SPINOZA BELIEVED THAT REASON BRINGS
blessedness not only to individuals but to society
as a whole. In his view, conflicts among people
arise only when individuals allow themselves to
be ruled by their passions. If people pursued the
life of reason instead, they would be guided to
do only what is good for human nature, which is
everywhere and always the same, and it would be
obvious that what benefits the individual benefits
everyone else as well. A society of truly right-
minded people living under the guidance of reason
would need no laws or government at all to control
their interactions.

Unfortunately, Spinoza's vision of a
harmonious, self-regulated, and rational world was
far from reality in the Dutch Republic during the
fall of 1665. Day by day, the forces of intolerance

and superstition seemed to be growing stronger. On the local level, the conflict over the appointment of a new pastor in Voorburg had turned downright nasty. Spinoza, associated in the public mind with the more liberal candidate, was increasingly the target of vicious insults—especially the damning one of being an atheist, which one accuser defined, rather ominously, as "a man who mocks all religions and is thus a pernicious element in this republic."

The conflict in Voorburg was a miniature version of the Dutch Republic's divide between open-minded and closed-minded forces. The merchant oligarchy was still in charge, and its generally tolerant policies were still in place. The period was still rightfully known as the "True Freedom," the name proudly given to it by the most powerful man in the Republic, the grand pensionary Johan de Witt—essentially the country's prime minister. But the war with England, especially the prospect of William III becoming stadtholder, was stoking the tensions between the two camps. While the merchant oligarchy wanted England to suffer a decisive and crushing defeat, the Dutch Reformed Church was interested in establishing good relations with England as soon as possible. Calvinist opposition to De Witt and his True Freedom was growing stronger and more strident.

JOHAN DE WITT:
Aside from being a statesman, Johan de Witt was an accomplished mathematician who wrote an early textbook on analytic geometry. He is memorialized by statues in his hometown of Dordrecht and in The Hague.

Jan de Witt by Lambert Visscher, probably 1633–1690 or after. Courtesy of the National Gallery of Art, Washington.

The Dutch Reformed Church enjoyed widespread popular support. Most people, after all, were not members of the merchant elite and did not share that class's priorities. But even more importantly, most people were not especially interested in questioning the traditions in which they had been raised. By and large, they were faithful churchgoers accustomed to viewing their religious leaders as authoritative guides to the way a good Christian should think, believe, and act. And religious leaders were certainly outspoken about those matters. During church services, the *predikanten* did not hesitate to make clear which political, social, and economic positions smoothed the way to heaven and which ones paved the way to hell.

For Spinoza, as well as for anyone else who valued religious and intellectual freedom, the situation was genuinely alarming. The *predikanten* could easily mobilize the general population in their effort to gain political and spiritual control over the Dutch Republic. It was nothing less than a war between the forces of tolerance and intolerance, and most of the foot soldiers were being manipulated by superstitions and fears shamelessly fostered by religious leaders.

Local and national events in the Dutch Republic demonstrated how easily religious leaders could lead the masses into complete irrationality. If any further proof was necessary, the Jewish world provided it. Although he no longer identified himself as a Jew, Spinoza could hardly have remained ignorant of a frenzy that had seized Jewish communities throughout the Middle East and Europe and stirred up many Christians as well. In the early months of 1665, a charismatic but emotionally unstable Turkish-born Jew, Sabbatai Zevi, had declared himself to be the messiah. The messiah, according to traditional Jewish belief, would be the savior sent by God to gather together the scattered Jewish nation and lead it back to its rightful home in the Holy Land. Zevi had announced that this final redemption of the Jewish people would take place the following year, on June 18, 1666.

Word of the final redemption spread with lightning speed, and Zevi attracted an enormous following. By November 1665, the Jewish community of Amsterdam was in turmoil. Members of the Nation danced riotously in public streets, ignoring the usual concern about offending non-Jewish neighbors, and in their certainty that Jews the world over were about to be united for their return to the Holy Land, they began to shake off their usual commitments. Merchants ignored their businesses and homeowners sold their property, even at a terrible financial loss. The community even

Waare afbeeldinge van Sabetha Sebi den genaemden
herſteller des Joodtſchen Rijcks.
Vrai pourtrait de Sabbathai Sevi qui ſe dict Restaura-
teur du Royaume de Juda & Jſrael.

SABBATAI ZEVI: Hebrew inscriptions in the background refer to biblical prophecies about the messiah, and Zevi is presumably pointing to one of those passages. The legend at the bottom reads, "True portrait of Sabbatai Zevi, self-proclaimed restorer of the Kingdom of Judah and Israel."

Frontispiece from Thomas Coenen's *Ydele verwachtinge der Joden getoont in den persoon van Sabethai Zevi* (Amsterdam, 1669). Rare Book and Manuscript Library, Columbia University in the City of New York.

made plans to dig up the Jewish cemetery so that the bones of the dead could make the move along with the living.

With their tortured history, the Jews of Amsterdam were especially prone to believe Sabbatai Zevi's declaration that the final redemption was at hand. Surely God had some kind of plan for healing their wounds and for ending the torment of Jews still trapped in Spain and Portugal. Jews in other places, who had suffered tribulations of their own and by now held Amsterdam's Jewish community in high esteem, also got caught up in the whirlwind. It was the rare Jewish community that remained unaffected. And many Christians, who eagerly awaited their own messiah, were excited as well. In their minds, the Jewish redemption and the Second Coming of Christ were closely linked, if not identical.

It all ended in nothing, and it did so quite abruptly. In February 1666, Zevi was arrested and imprisoned by Turkish authorities for the disruptions caused by his messianic activities, and he was given the choice of death or conversion to Islam. He chose conversion. His betrayal of Judaism left his followers bewildered and bitter. Their would-be messiah had dashed their dreams and left them to pick up the scattered pieces of their lives.

Even before the inevitable crash, the whole episode could only confirm Spinoza's views of traditional religions and their leaders. Hordes of gullible people had been swept into an insane frenzy because of a fairy tale that had nothing to do with true religion. The frenzy had been encouraged not only by the self-appointed messiah who had begun the whole thing but also by the local religious leaders who had fanned the messianic fervor of their flocks. In the process, people had suspended their ability to think clearly and rationally—the ability that makes all of us truly human.

And so, in the fall of 1665, Spinoza interrupted his work on the *Ethics* to address a more immediate concern. Before people could even begin to embark on reason's path to blessedness, they needed to shed the chains of unreason that bound them. Traditional religions needed to be exposed for what they genuinely were—combinations of superstition and myth—and religious leaders needed to be exposed for what *they* genuinely were—power-hungry individuals eager to take advantage of the naïve masses. And the freedom to think independently and the right to publicize one's views needed to be championed with all the force that Spinoza could muster. It needed to be absolutely clear that those freedoms are not only harmless to the welfare of a country but absolutely essential to its health.

The new project occupied most of Spinoza's attention until 1670. Only then did Spinoza resume work on the *Ethics*, but he did not live to see the publication of his philosophical masterpiece. Yet the project for which Spinoza interrupted his work on the *Ethics* would become one of the most explosive books ever to emerge in the history of European thought.

CHAPTER TWENTY-ONE

THE *THEOLOGICAL-POLITICAL TREATISE*

SPINOZA FELT A REAL SENSE OF MISSION AS HE embarked on his new project, which he eventually named the *Theological-Political Treatise.* "Theological" means "relating to the study of God or religion," and much of the book examines, step by step, some of the core beliefs of the Judeo-Christian tradition. Spinoza's goal was to separate what he considered true religion from what he considered the absurd superstition of most established religions. His first step in achieving this goal was to show that the things that traditional religions wrap in mystery can be understood in perfectly natural ways.

Spinoza starts by completely rejecting the notion of revealed religion—that God or God's messenger somehow came down from on high to reveal the true form of religion to human beings.

Instead, claims Spinoza, religions are entirely man-made. Because people feel helpless in the face of the unknowable future, they imagine that some kind of supernatural power is in charge, and they do whatever they can to please that power. They may pray, offer gifts, or make sacrifices—whatever they think will bring about the results they desire. These practices become the basic rituals of religion, but they do not stand on a firm footing because people are extremely inconstant. As soon as people get what they want, they stop trying to please the power that supposedly responded to their rituals.

Self-proclaimed religious leaders try to make beliefs and practices more permanent by clothing them in as much pageantry as possible. Pageantry leaves a strong impression on the minds of common people, who as a result become more constant in their ritual observances. Houses of worship are built and formal services are organized, and the leader's position—including emotional, intellectual, and physical control over the people—becomes more established. Religious leaders also work to gain political power so that any departures from the now-established religion can be considered a crime against the state. From this process emerges an organized system of belief and practice that is based on superstition and mindless devotion to religious leaders. This system has absolutely nothing to do with true religion.

With the same goal of showing that supernatural notions really originate in very natural experiences, Spinoza addresses, one by one, some of the core beliefs of the Judeo-Christian tradition. In rapid succession, he tears down the mystery surrounding prophets, the Jewish people, ritual, and miracles. The prophets were unique not because of a magical ability to communicate with God or to know what science had not yet revealed but because they had highly developed imaginations. The biblical term "Chosen People" refers not to any supposed spiritual uniqueness of Jews throughout the ages but to the worldly situation of the ancient Israelites, who at a specific point in their history benefited from their excellent social organization and political good fortune. The Bible established rituals and commandments not because they have any eternal or mystical relevance but because they were necessary to maintain a particular society's lifestyle at a particular point in time. And finally, miracles do not exist. Ancient people called something a miracle when they did not understand the natural causes behind what they were experiencing. Even when the natural cause was understood, the Bible sometimes presented an event as a miracle in order to secure the interest and devotion of ordinary people.

The Bible, too, undergoes Spinoza's demystifying analysis. The Bible is simply a human book—an immensely profound one, with a great deal to say about moral behavior—but human all the same. It was authored by people, not by God, and even the Five Books of Moses were not written by Moses. The Bible's frequent repetitions, anachronisms, and inconsistencies show that the text was in fact composed by a variety of writers and editors over a long period of time.

The Bible must therefore be read in the same way as any other book—with an excellent grasp of its language and a solid understanding of the historical and cultural environments in which its authors lived. No preconceived notions, whether about the Bible's origins, holiness, or meaning, should be brought to its study, and there is absolutely no need for outside religious authorities to provide specially authorized interpretations. "I hold that the method of interpreting Scripture is no different from the method of interpreting Nature," declared Spinoza. Just like the new science, a proper approach to the Bible rejects any religious traditions or supernatural assumptions and draws conclusions strictly from the material under study.

A correct reading, free of any preconceptions, demonstrates that the Bible is a guide to ethical behavior, not a source of scientific truth. If we want to know how to live wholesomely and interact appropriately with others, the Bible is a suitable resource. But if we want to know how the natural world functions, there is absolutely no substitute for human reason. It is absurd to deny the truths of science when they contradict the Bible, and it is pointless to try to harmonize the results of scientific and biblical inquiry. Science and the Bible are entirely different domains with entirely different goals.

And, as a guide to appropriate behavior, the Bible shows that the only thing that really matters is the simple moral core of the true, universal religion, which consists in loving our fellow human beings and in loving God—which, for Spinoza, though he does not say so here, really means understanding our place within nature. The truth is that one can arrive at this understanding just by using the faculty of reason, without consulting the Bible at all. But since most people are not philosophers, the Bible plays an extremely important role in helping people lead morally upright lives.

At this point, Spinoza introduces the argument for tolerance to which he has been leading all along. True religion is free of all things but the most basic moral behavior, and anything beyond that is completely optional. Individuals who find specific rituals and beliefs helpful in leading a moral life are welcome to take them on—but not to insist that others do so as well. No one has the right to interfere with another person's freedom to think through these issues and arrive at conclusions independently.

After stripping away the myths and superstitions of traditional religions, Spinoza turns to the more purely political part of his *Theological-Political Treatise*. Here, too, there were plenty of mystical notions to strip away. Most European countries of the time were monarchies, and, like the Calvinists who wanted the stadtholder restored, many people assumed that monarchy had the Bible's stamp of approval. Monarchs themselves were happy to promote the idea of the divine right of kings—the idea that human rulers receive the right to rule directly from God.

To strip away such misguided ideas, Spinoza does for government exactly what he did for religion: he presents a natural account of how the institution first came to be. In a state of nature, he explains, before mankind has developed codes of morality, religion, or government, human beings are completely justified in doing whatever they feel is in their self-interest. If someone else owns something that I think I need, for instance, I am entitled to steal that thing or to kill its owner. This, of course, is a rather unpleasant and dangerous way to live, so people quickly reach the obvious conclusion: for the greater good of all, everyone needs to restrain his or her acts of self-interest. People therefore agree to transfer their natural right to a specific ruling body, whether a monarchy, an oligarchy, or a democracy. This man-made ruling body now has all the power that once belonged to individuals, and it can threaten with dire punishment anyone who tries to break the agreement.

Although individuals emerging from the state of nature can form different kinds of ruling bodies, not all ruling bodies are equally good. Democracy is by far the best because it most accurately reflects the will of the entire group that has formed it and is least likely to abuse its power. Furthermore, a democracy is most likely to base its decisions on reason. Because a democratic government consists of many members, the inevitable excesses or misguidedness of specific individuals will always be balanced out by the more reasonable tendencies of others. Monarchy is at the opposite end of the spectrum. Monarchy is the least likely to reflect the will of the entire group, the least likely to base its decisions on reason, and the most likely to abuse its power.

No matter what form of government is established, it holds *all* the power to decide what serves the public good in a given society. This means that religious leaders do not have any such right. When religious leaders claim the right to determine public policy, they are competing for power that rightfully belongs to the government, and the stability of the country suffers as a result of the competition.

On the flip side of the coin, the government's exclusive power over all public matters includes the right to determine the outward expression of religion, such as public worship, ceremonies, and rituals. By no means, however, does the government have power over the inward expression of religion or the beliefs and opinions of individual citizens. These matters, which have nothing to do with the basic, universal core of true religion, are at the individual's discretion. Even if the government wanted to control beliefs and opinions, it would be unable to do so, since no one can control another person's thoughts. For that matter, it is virtually impossible for the government to control the public expression of those thoughts, since people will always find a way to say what they think.

Not only is it futile for the government to seek control over thought and speech, it is counterproductive and even dangerous. The attempt to suppress personal judgment and punish its free expression discourages progress in the arts and sciences and leads to wicked behavior by those who feel oppressed—in other words, it prevents people from reaching their full potential.

The various topics that Spinoza explores in the *Theological-Political Treatise* build up to this final, passionate point: freedom of thought and freedom of expression are the inalienable rights of individuals, whose ability to use their own reason is what makes them fully human. These sacred freedoms must be upheld by the government. Spinoza insists that the "real disturbers of peace are those who, in a free commonwealth, vainly seek to abolish freedom of judgment, which cannot be suppressed."

Spinoza made only occasional reference to current events in the Dutch Republic, but in the *Theological-Political Treatise* he was obviously staking out a specific political position for his time and place. His writing was a scathing attack on the Calvinists who sought to restore a monarchical form of government and use political power to control the intellectual and spiritual lives of all citizens. And the book was a powerful statement of support for De Witt's True Freedom. The intolerant forces threatening to overrun the country could be countered only by an unwavering guarantee of free thought and expression.

CHAPTER TWENTY-TWO

URGENT REASONS
TO PUBLISH

ANYONE WHO READS THE *ETHICS* AND THE
Theological-Political Treatise is struck by the
different feel of the two works. The *Ethics* proceeds
in a stately, impersonal way, like the geometric
proofs upon which it is modeled. It is hard to get
a feel for the author behind the carefully selected
words, which, like the language of mathematics,
are direct and unadorned, calculated to avoid any
hint of excess. By contrast, the *Theological-Political
Treatise* feels downright autobiographical. It is not
that Spinoza speaks about himself—he almost
never does in any of his philosophical writings.
It is instead that Spinoza breaks free of a rigidly
controlled format and gives a more spontaneous
expression to his feelings. His fury at religious
leaders who meddle in government and his passion

for the freedom to philosophize come through loudly and clearly.

Spinoza's outrage and sense of mission could only have deepened during the approximately four years it took him to complete the work. First was the news that Henry Oldenburg had been arrested and imprisoned in the Tower of London during the summer of 1667. Oldenburg's crime, apparently, was to have criticized Charles II and complained about the way that England was conducting the war against the Dutch Republic. Spinoza was on the opposite side of the conflict and would not have sympathized with the specifics of Oldenburg's position. But Spinoza certainly did not believe that Oldenburg belonged in prison. No person should end up in jail for expressing his or her opinions.

Oldenburg was released once the war had ended, after he had spent about two months in prison. He emerged in a significantly weakened state, both physically and financially, and he worried about his ability to continue his work for the Royal Society. But compared to another friend of Spinoza's, Oldenburg came out magnificently.

This friend was Adriaan Koerbagh, who had been a member of the Cartesian circle many years earlier in Amsterdam. Koerbagh had little respect for organized religions or their rituals. He believed that the Bible was composed by human beings and that its study requires the same tools that one would use to study any other text—a thorough familiarity with its language and its historical and cultural background. Religious authorities have no special access to the Bible's meaning because anyone with the use of reason can read the Bible adequately. True religion involves nothing more than the knowledge and love of God and the love of fellow human beings. Democracy is the best form of government, and religious authorities need to be kept out of politics. God and nature are one and the same, and everything results from nature's long chains of cause and effect.

Koerbagh's views should sound quite familiar since they were virtually the same as Spinoza's. What the two men did not share, however, was personality. Spinoza led a quiet life whose simple decency even his harshest critics acknowledged. But Koerbagh was unrestrained. He had had a child out of wedlock and had been officially rebuked by the *predikanten* for his immoral behavior. And he did not share Spinoza's concern for caution. In writing and publicizing his work, Koerbagh was exuberantly provocative.

In 1668, Koerbagh published a book with a title that certainly seemed wholesome enough—*A Flower Garden Composed of All Kinds of Loveliness.* The book's stated purpose, to explain the many foreign words that had made their way into Dutch, seemed just as wholesome as the title. But a sampling of Koerbagh's definitions demonstrates quite clearly that his intentions were far from innocent. His definition of the word "altar," for instance, describes a physical structure around which priests can engage in a "marvelous affair, that is, in the creation of a human being. For they can do what even God cannot do, at any hour of the day: make a human creature from a small piece of wheatcake. . . . What an absurdity!" Koerbagh was obviously mocking the Christian rite of the Eucharist, in which the body of Jesus is associated with a wafer or another form of bread. In his definition of the word "Bible," Koerbagh wrote that there is "in Scripture, something that is certain and that agrees with reason. . . . But the rest is, for us, useless and vain, and can be rejected without difficulty."

Beneath Koerbagh's sneers was a serious point with which Spinoza wholeheartedly agreed. Indeed, it was one of the major ideas at the heart of the *Theological-Political Treatise*. Organized religions create auras of impenetrable mystery around ritual and the Bible. As a result, the stature of religious leaders—the people in charge of all this mystery— becomes ever more secure, and regular people are prevented from using their own minds to make sense of things. But Koerbagh was making the point in a way that was calculated to scandalize traditional thinkers—and he deliberately published the book in Dutch, not Latin, so that it could be read by as many people as possible in the Dutch Republic.

The outrage of the Dutch Reformed Church was to be expected. But Koerbagh was so provocative that he infuriated even the more liberal political establishment. What would become of public morality if such ideas were allowed to circulate among the general population? When later that same year Koerbagh attempted to have a second book published—another work critical of established religions and of specific Christian beliefs, including the divinity of Jesus—his frightened printer notified the authorities. Koerbagh attempted to flee but was soon caught.

At his trial in Amsterdam, Koerbagh was asked, among other things, about his connection with Spinoza. This was both interesting and alarming. Up to this point, Spinoza had published only *Descartes's Principles of Philosophy* and the *Metaphysical Thoughts*, the double volume that had won him a solid reputation as a Cartesian expert. None of Spinoza's other works had been made public. He had temporarily set aside his work on the *Ethics*, he was in the middle of writing the *Theological-Political Treatise*, and he had circulated his first two treatises only among his closest friends.

Yet his views were sufficiently well-known—and notorious—for his connection with Koerbagh to concern the officials. And given that his views were nearly identical to Koerbagh's, Spinoza could just as easily have been on trial himself.

On July 29, 1668, Koerbagh was sentenced to ten years in prison, to be followed by ten years in exile. He was also charged a fine of four thousand guilders—the equivalent of over twenty-seven years of wages for a skilled worker. This was actually the gentle sentence. Another member of the judicial committee had recommended cutting off Koerbagh's right thumb, piercing his tongue with a red-hot iron, imprisoning him for thirty years, confiscating all his property, and burning all his books. As it turned out, however, the lighter sentence was heavy enough. Koerbagh's health deteriorated rapidly in the harsh conditions of prison, and he was dead within a year and three months of his sentencing.

True Freedom was in desperate trouble, and the need to uphold free thought and expression was more important than ever. Spinoza was now determined to battle the forces of intolerance with the arguments of reason. But this was a dangerous game. If he published the *Theological-Political Treatise*, he could easily find himself suffering the same fate as his unfortunate friend.

The only solution was to proceed with as much caution as possible. After putting the finishing touches on the *Theological-Political Treatise*, Spinoza brought the manuscript to Amsterdam, where he delivered it to his trusted friend Jan Rieuwertsz, the printer and bookseller. Rieuwertsz, who had published Spinoza's work on Descartes, was happy to be involved in another of Spinoza's projects—and was unfazed by the genuine danger this time around. Rieuwertsz never hesitated to publish radical writings, but he shrewdly avoided unnecessary trouble. He and Spinoza agreed that the published book would contain no mention of the author's name and that the name of the publisher and place of printing would be falsified.

And so the *Theological-Political Treatise* came out in early 1670, its title page announcing that the book had been printed in Hamburg by Henricum Kunrath. Although Henricum Kunrath had been a real person—a German alchemist and member of a secret philosophical society in the second half of the sixteenth century—there was certainly no printer by that name in Hamburg during the mid-1600s. And, of course, Spinoza's name appeared nowhere in the book.

With these precautions in place and his work beginning to circulate publicly, Spinoza eagerly waited for his passionate defense of tolerance to do

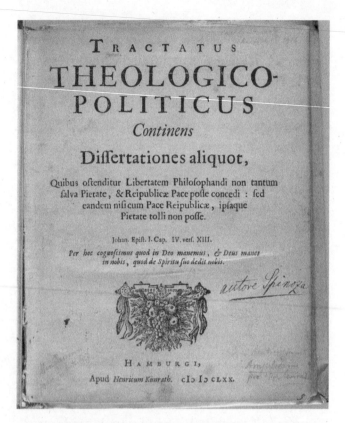

TRACTATUS

THEOLOGICO-
POLITICUS

Continens

Diſſertationes aliquot,

Quibus oſtenditur Libertatem Philoſophandi non tantum
ſalva Pietate, & Reipublicæ Pace poſſe concedi : ſed
eandem niſi cum Pace Reipublicæ, ipſaque
Pietate tolli non poſſe.

Johan. Epiſt. I. Cap. IV. verſ. XIII.

*Per hoc cognoſcimus quod in Deo manemus, & Deus manet
in nobis, quod de Spiritu ſuo dedit nobis.*

HAMBURGI,

Apud *Henricum Kunrath.* cIɔ Iɔ cLxx.

THE *THEOLOGICAL-POLITICAL TREATISE*: This title page
misleadingly identifies the city of publication as Hamburg and the
publisher as Henricum Kunrath. Spinoza's name is not printed at all,
and its absence seems to have led an early owner or cataloguer of the
book to pen in the words *autore* [author] *Spinoza*. The long subtitle
summarizes Spinoza's ultimate argument in the work: "Containing
Various Disquisitions, By means of which it is shown not only that
Freedom of Philosophising can be allowed in Preserving Piety and the
Peace of the Republic: but also that it is not possible for such Freedom
to be upheld except when accompanied by the Peace of the Republic
and Piety Themselves."

Title page of *Tractatus theologico-politicus. Cui adjunctus est Philosophia
S. Scripturæ interpres*, 1670. Rare Book and Manuscript Library,
Columbia University in the City of New York.

its work. He had enormous faith in the power of reason to overcome irrationality and superstition, and he had high hopes that his arguments would prove effective—so effective, in fact, that he would soon be able to publish the *Ethics*, which he considered even more radical than the *Theological-Political Treatise*.

The anonymous authorship and false publishing information may have temporarily protected Spinoza and Rieuwertsz, but it did not take long before the true identities of the author and publisher were widely known. That neither of them shared Koerbagh's fate was probably the result of two factors: Spinoza had written his book in Latin, which seriously limited the number of people who could read it, and Spinoza's style, although intense and outspoken, did not have the sneering quality of Koerbagh's. Nonetheless, Spinoza was grossly mistaken in his hopes for the *Theological-Political Treatise*.

CHAPTER TWENTY-THREE

THE FURIOUS
PUBLIC RESPONSE

IT WAS PROBABLY FORTUNATE THAT SPINOZA MOVED
out of contentious little Voorburg at just about the
time that the *Theological-Political Treatise* made its
public appearance. Spinoza moved to The Hague,
home to a more diverse population and a livelier
intellectual life. Additionally, as the political capital
of both the province and the country, The Hague
was the epicenter of the True Freedom—at least for
the time being.

It was at the urging of Spinoza's many friends
and connections in The Hague that he made the
move. He found a comfortable set of third-story
rooms in the home of a recently widowed woman,
and there he maintained the usual industrious
quiet of his life. Although he welcomed visitors
from time to time and occasionally made visits
of his own into the city center, he mostly kept

to himself. The widow generally served meals to her lodgers in the dining room, but Spinoza often preferred to eat in his own rooms. Sometimes he kept himself so busy with his reading, writing, and lens grinding that he did not emerge for several days at a time. After about a year, Spinoza moved from the widow's house to smaller and less expensive lodgings in the nearby home of Hendrik and Ida van der Spyck. Spinoza's personal finances were never robust, and he needed to keep his expenses as low as possible.

Spinoza's retiring lifestyle could not have contrasted more sharply with the storm that raged around his recently published book. The response was immediate and scathing, but at least for the first few months—before the anonymous author was identified with any certainty—the attacks did not target Spinoza personally. Most surprising was just how universally the *Theological-Political Treatise* was condemned. The fury spread far beyond the Calvinists, extending even to groups Spinoza might have considered natural allies in his call for tolerance.

Of course, it took almost no time for the Calvinists to launch their offensive. By April 1670, just a few months after the book made its appearance, church committees in major cities began to demand that all sale of the *Treatise* be

halted and all existing copies seized and suppressed.
Religious leaders in the city of Utrecht were first
to make this demand, but they were soon joined
by their colleagues in Leiden, Haarlem, and
Amsterdam. These committees freely hurled abuse
at the book, whose wickedness they considered
beyond dispute. The *Treatise* was "profane" and
"blasphemous," it contained "monstrosities" and
"obscenities," and it would destroy the moral fabric
of society.

By the summer, the religious protest against
the book was swelling from the cities to the larger
district levels of the Dutch Reformed Church. The
outrage was relentless. According to one district,
the *Treatise* was "as obscene and blasphemous a
book as, to our knowledge, the world has ever seen."
The *predikanten* called for immediate suppression
of the work, but the church itself was powerless to
take any real action. By law, only political authorities
could halt the book's printing, prohibit its sale, or
raid bookstores to seize existing copies. The various
church districts joined together to pressure the
national government into action.

But the national government moved slowly, since
any new measure had to work its long way through
the judicial and legislative systems. Some of the
more liberal-minded officials may also have dragged
their feet intentionally, and in this they would have

been aided by the *Treatise*'s falsified and missing publication information. At least for a time, officials reluctant to ban the book could claim that they had not yet succeeded in identifying the scoundrels behind it. The truth, however, is that most political figures were not well disposed to the *Treatise*, and descriptions of the book as "slanderous" and "soul-corrupting" came even from governmental quarters. For the most part, though, even the more alarmed politicians preferred to keep things quiet. After all, banning a book is often the best way to increase its popularity.

Church officials, enraged by the slow-moving national government, focused instead on targets closer to hand. Working with local officials, *predikanten* successfully banned the *Treatise* in their own communities and towns. All around them, they claimed, were ominous signs of the book's terrible impact. Amsterdam's religious leaders blamed the *Treatise*, along with a couple of other books—one written by Spinoza's friend Lodewijk Meyer—for "the increase of cry-aloud-to-heaven transgressions, slanders of God's name, blasphemies, curses, Sabbath-shaming, desecrations, contempt of religion, dishonor, and such." God's inescapable punishment for all this evil was on its way: "the almighty God will issue his anger from heaven; and already the appearance of his anger pours upon our dear fatherland."

Local censorship drove Rieuwertsz to more extensive trickery in later editions of the *Treatise*. On one occasion he bound Spinoza's book together with Meyer's and gave the combined volume the title *Complete Surgical Writings by Francisco Henriquez de Villacorta, Medical Doctor*, a book supposedly "printed with permission of Spanish King Charles II and published in Amsterdam by 'J. Paulli.'" On another occasion, the *Treatise* appeared in the *Collection of the Historical Works of Daniel Heinsius*.

Far more irritating to Spinoza than the Calvinists' predictable condemnation was the unexpectedly harsh reaction from intellectuals and liberal Protestants. The first published attack on the *Treatise* came, in fact, not from the Dutch Reformed Church but from Jakob Thomasius, a German professor of philosophy, law, and theology who bestowed the damning description "atheist" upon the as-yet unidentified author of the *Treatise*. Thomasius called the work "a godless document" that should be immediately banned in every country.

Another early response came from Willem van Blijenbergh, the correspondent whom Spinoza had entirely misjudged as a fellow spirit. If the difference between the two men had not become completely clear nine years earlier, Blijenbergh's five-hundred-page response to the *Treatise* would have ably done the job. The basic thrust of Blijenbergh's response is adequately revealed by his characteristically long title: *The Truth of the Christian Religion and the Authority of the Holy Scripture Affirmed Against the Arguments of the Impious, or A Refutation of the Blasphemous Book Titled "Theological-Political Treatise."*

But the likes of Thomasius and Blijenbergh were not the real problem. Even among professional academics and self-styled intellectuals, there would always be narrow-minded individuals. What was infuriating was the response of people who should have understood from their own experience the importance of a book like the *Theological-Political Treatise*—people who had a genuine stake in a more tolerant society. Spinoza had anticipated support from thinkers committed to Cartesianism and the new science, Collegiants looking for the true core of religion amidst beliefs and rituals they rejected, political figures at the heart of the True Freedom. But even large numbers of those people expressed horror at Spinoza's views.

When Henry Oldenburg, for instance, discovered who had written the *Treatise*, he sent Spinoza a harshly worded letter that may explain a long breakdown in their communication. Only after Oldenburg sent Spinoza a sincere apology— more than five years after the first appearance of the *Treatise*—did the two men resume their correspondence. As secretary of the Royal Society, committed to nurturing new science throughout Europe—not to mention as someone who had himself been jailed for expressing his political opinions—Oldenburg might have recognized the obstacles posed by intolerant traditionalists. But instead of applauding Spinoza's insistence on freedom of thought and expression, Oldenburg drew back in alarm.

The most hurtful responses came from prominent Cartesian thinkers. Lambert van Velthuysen, for example, had gotten into trouble with religious authorities for promoting Cartesian philosophy and the sun-centered planetary system. And yet Van Velthuysen found in the *Treatise* an intolerable attack on religion. In 1671 he wrote to a friend, "I think I have not strayed far from the truth, nor am I unfair to the author, if I denounce him as teaching sheer atheism with furtive and disguised arguments." When the recipient forwarded the letter to Spinoza, Spinoza reacted with an uncharacteristic irritability. "I can hardly bring myself to answer that man's letter," he responded.

Even Johan de Witt found Spinoza's ideas too extreme for his taste—and this was particularly discouraging because one of the reasons Spinoza had undertaken the *Treatise* was to strengthen De

Witt's faltering True Freedom. De Witt did not know what Spinoza had written about God in the as-yet incomplete *Ethics*, but it was already clear in the *Treatise* that Spinoza's God was not a transcendent power that metes out reward and punishment to the human species. Like so many others of his day, De Witt could not fathom why the vast majority of people would bother to behave morally without the promise of reward or the threat of punishment. The *Treatise*, as De Witt saw it, posed a real threat to the fabric of society. When Spinoza heard of De Witt's disapproval, he resolved to arrange a personal meeting and sent someone to request an interview. The philosopher received a blunt answer: "his excellency did not want to see him pass his threshold."

It was clear to just about everyone that Spinoza was the worst of villains and that his book was the vilest of perversions. In a list of the books owned by De Witt when he died, the cataloguer expressed the prevailing view in his entry for the *Treatise*: "Forged in hell by the apostate Jew working together with the devil."

CHAPTER TWENTY-FOUR

TRUE FREEDOM'S
GORY END

THE SITUATION WOULD GET WORSE BEFORE IT GOT
better. In 1671, Spinoza was startled by the news
that his well-meaning Amsterdam friends had
commissioned a Dutch translation of the *Treatise*
and were already making plans to publish it.
Without doubt, a Dutch translation would inflame
the situation. An immediate banning of the work,
even in its Latin version, would certainly result, and
the consequences for Spinoza, whose identity as the
author of the *Treatise* was by now well known, could
be deadly. Spinoza immediately wrote to his friends
in Amsterdam to halt the process. The Dutch
translation would not appear for more than twenty
years, long after Spinoza's death.

And then De Witt's True Freedom came to
a sickening and terrifying end. The year 1672
was the worst that anyone could remember, even

considering the eighty-year war with Spain and the constant outbreak of tensions with England. In 1672, the Dutch Republic found itself attacked not only by England but also by France, which had long wanted to expand its territory into the southern Netherlands. To make matters worse, those two major powers were joined by the German states of Cologne and Münster just to the east. The overwhelmed Dutch Republic, surrounded by enemies, lost a great deal of territory to the invading armies.

The state of affairs was so bad that 1672 became known in Dutch history as the *Rampjaar*—the Disaster Year—and a well-known saying describes the population of the time as *redeloos* (irrational), the government as *radeloos* (desperate), and the entire country as *reddeloos* (beyond rescue). People wanted a scapegoat, and Johan de Witt, always under attack by the influential Calvinist clergy, was the obvious target. Legitimate disputes over his policies were supplemented by false charges publicized in anonymous pamphlets. De Witt, according to the accusations, had stolen public money for his private use and was even planning to hand the Republic over to its enemies so that he could rule it on their behalf.

On the way home from his office in The Hague one night in June, De Witt was attacked by a group of four men, at least one of whom carried a knife; all four were well-educated individuals from reputable families. De Witt's wounds were not serious, but it was several weeks before he resumed his official responsibilities. His recovery period, however, only increased public outcry against his allegedly feeble leadership. In July, the Calvinists finally scored their long-sought victory: William III was installed as stadtholder. De Witt resigned his office as grand pensionary in early August.

But even these changes were not enough to satisfy the people's need for a scapegoat. Public rage against De Witt had spread to his brother, Cornelis, who had been imprisoned since July on false charges of attempting to assassinate William III. Cornelis was officially cleared of the accusation on August 20, and he was free to leave prison. De Witt, concerned that Cornelis needed assistance to leave safely, rushed to his brother's side. In the meantime, supporters of William III, furious that the charges had been dropped, stirred up an angry mob right outside the prison gate.

As soon as the brothers stepped outside the gate, the maddened masses, yelling "Traitors!" surged against them. The De Witts were forced back behind the gate, where at least they were protected by the armed soldiers posted at the prison walls. But soon the soldiers were called away to deal with another issue on the outskirts of the city. When the commander received the order to move his troops, he remarked, "I shall obey, but now the De Witts are dead men." He was right.

The mob broke through the now unguarded gate and stormed in, finding the De Witt brothers quietly reading in one of the cells. The two men were triumphantly seized by the impatient and bloodthirsty throng. The original plan had been to hang them, but they did not survive the abuse long enough to get to the scaffold. The disappointed attackers cruelly improvised. They stripped the bodies naked, hung them by the feet, and dismembered much of what was left. Body parts and bits of flesh were sold as souvenirs or roasted on the spot and eaten.

Many of the people involved in the horrifying incident were otherwise respectable, upstanding citizens. Passion had overrun any commitment to reason, to balance, to law—to everything that distinguishes human society from a pack of wild animals. The night after the murders, the sickened Spinoza prepared a sign reading *Ultimi barbarorum* (the greatest of barbarians) to post near the site of the massacre. But Hendrik van der Spyck, Spinoza's landlord, barred the door and refused to let Spinoza out. Spinoza was known to support De Witt, and it was even rumored that De Witt had secretly coauthored the *Treatise* or, at the very least, had been

LYNCHING OF THE DE WITTS: Behind the furious mob depicted in the foreground of this etching, the naked bodies of the De Witt brothers hang upside down from the gallows. At the top are the portraits of Cornelis (left) and Johan (right).

Afbeelding en waarachtigh Verhaal . . . (Representation of the True Story of Johan de Witt . . .) by Romeyn de Hooghe, 1672. Courtesy of National Gallery of Art, Washington.

the one preventing the government from banning the book. Van der Spyck may have been chiefly concerned about the safety of his own family and property, but he almost certainly saved Spinoza's life that night.

True Freedom was dead. The country had shifted inexorably toward a less representational government and tighter controls on personal freedoms. Under Stadtholder William III's centralized rule, the Calvinists finally achieved their long-sought goal regarding the *Theological-Political Treatise*. In the summer of 1674, four-and-a-half years after it had first appeared in print, the book was officially banned in the Dutch Republic.

And if, at this point, Spinoza still looked for support from Cartesian philosophers, his likeliest intellectual allies, his hopes were quickly dashed. The Cartesians knew that they, too, were deeply mistrusted by the Dutch Reformed Church and that the crackdown on Spinoza could all too easily spread to them. Instead of seeing the attack on one person's freedom as the call to fight for everyone's freedom, the Cartesians chose to save their own skins. To distance themselves as much as possible from Spinoza, they attacked the *Treatise* more relentlessly and viciously than they had before the ban. Spinoza complained to Oldenburg about the disgraceful tactic of the "stupid Cartesians," who, "in order to remove this suspicion from themselves because they are thought to be on my side, ceased not to denounce everywhere my opinions and my writings, and still continue to do so."

The forces of intolerance had won. Spinoza's stirring defense of freedom had fallen on deaf ears.

CHAPTER TWENTY-FIVE

QUIET AMIDST THE STORM

IT IS PROBABLY FAIR TO SAY THAT MANY PEOPLE would fall apart under the various stresses and disappointments that Spinoza faced almost everywhere he turned. He was despised, insulted, and deemed a poisonous influence on society. His book was banned and his message of tolerance ignored. His every move was monitored lest he attempt to publish yet another abominable, soul-eroding treatise. He might, at any moment, be brought to trial or attacked by a barbaric street mob. The real society in which he lived was hopelessly far from his ideal, and the gap was only growing larger. His mission had failed.

But Spinoza faced the situation with his usual self-possession. On one of his visits to a bookstore, he spotted a response to the *Treatise* written by Regnier van Mansvelt, a prominent Cartesian

professor at the University of Utrecht. It took only
a glance to see Mansvelt's predictable argument,
which was especially offensive because it was
coming from a Cartesian who should have known
better: the *Treatise* was harmful to all religions and
"ought to be buried forever in an eternal oblivion."
Spinoza calmly returned home and described his
reaction in a letter to a friend. "From the little that I
then read of it," Spinoza wrote, "I judged it not worth
reading through, and far less answering. So I left
the book lying there, and its author to remain such
as he was. I smiled as I reflected that the ignorant
are usually the most venturesome and most ready to
write."

In his quiet way of life, Spinoza found shelter
from the storm raging around him. His needs were
few, and in addition to the income from the lenses
he sold, he was now receiving an annual sum from
the estate of Simon Joosten de Vries, who had died
in 1667, leaving a deep void in Spinoza's circle of
close friends. De Vries had repeatedly attempted to
provide generous sums of money so that Spinoza
could live more comfortably, but Spinoza had
steadfastly refused his friend's offers. When De
Vries fell ill and realized that he was dying, he saw
his chance and made arrangements for Spinoza to
become his sole heir. But Spinoza, concerned that
De Vries's siblings would be denied an inheritance

that was rightfully theirs, would not hear of it, and he convinced his dying friend to change the terms of the will. Under the new terms, Spinoza would receive an annual allowance of 500 guilders. But even this Spinoza found excessive. After De Vries's death, Spinoza refused to accept more than 300 guilders a year from his friend's estate.

As always, Spinoza kept his personal needs to a minimum. He dressed plainly, ate modestly, and enjoyed simple pleasures. In the course of an entire day, he might eat only a single serving of humble milk soup or gruel, along with a bit of beer or wine to drink. When he felt the need to relax, he engaged in pleasant conversation with his housemates or played an occasional game of chess. For entertainment he watched the miniature but epic battles of spiders, which he initiated himself by pitting two of the creatures against each other or by throwing flies into webs. His most lavish and fashionable indulgences were smoking his pipe and sporting silver buckles on his shoes.

Spinoza got along extremely well with his landlord. Hendrik van der Spyck was an artist and painter, but he also did some work for the military. He and his wife, Ida, already had three small children when Spinoza moved in, and four more were born during the five-and-a-half years that Spinoza lived with them. Despite all the bustling activity, including the incessant patter of little feet on wooden floors, Spinoza found that he was able to concentrate on his work. Perhaps the flurried, beating life that surrounded him brought back memories of his own childhood.

Spinoza took great interest in the religious life of the Van der Spycks, who were devoted members of The Hague's Lutheran church. Lutheranism was widespread in Germany, but in the Dutch Republic it was decidedly in the minority. The denomination differed from Calvinism in various ways, but the most prominent difference was that Lutherans viewed the pleasures of this world as gifts of God to be enjoyed innocently and thankfully, while Calvinists abhorred the things of this world as snares of the devil. Spinoza had great respect for The Hague's Lutheran minister. He occasionally went to hear the minister himself, and he encouraged the Van der Spycks and his fellow lodgers not to miss any sermons by so excellent a preacher. And whenever the Van der Spycks returned home from church, Spinoza faithfully asked about what the minister had said.

But the man who lived so quietly in a corner of The Hague was by no means cut off from the larger world. Amidst all the public denunciation, Spinoza was gaining an underground following. Relentless condemnation of the *Treatise* kept the notorious book and its author in the public's attention, and Rieuwertsz's wily publishing tricks, along with the freethinking tendencies of various booksellers, meant that sufficiently determined and informed individuals could almost always find an illegal copy. The philosopher's circle of admirers in Amsterdam was expanding, already opening its doors to a second generation, and secret societies devoted to the study of Spinoza's ideas began to form elsewhere in the Republic as well as throughout Europe. A steady stream of visitors and letters regularly made its way to Spinoza's humble lodgings at the Van der Spycks'.

Spinoza must have sighed at some of the people who sought him out. There were the idly curious, those for whom celebrity was an irresistible attraction and with whom Spinoza had little in common, and the young, upper-class ladies eager to demonstrate their unusual intellectual attainments. The never-ending barrage of letters asked about all manner of things. On one occasion Spinoza found himself responding to a man who wanted to know whether or not he believed in ghosts. Ghosts may seem silly to us today, but for many seventeenth-century Europeans they were integral to the supernatural religious order that included the angels of heaven and the demons of hell. Spinoza had little patience for the question.

When his correspondent earnestly contrasted his certainty that there are male ghosts with his doubt that there are female ghosts, Spinoza responded with acidic mockery: "I am surprised that those who have seen naked spirits have not cast their eyes on the genital parts; perhaps they were too afraid, or ignorant of the difference."

Fortunately, there were also interactions that Spinoza found more to his taste. In February 1673, Spinoza received an intriguing letter from a representative of the German prince Karl Ludwig, the elector of Palatine. Karl Ludwig was a well-read and broad-minded man, and he was intent on making the University of Heidelberg, which was within his domain, one of the great universities of Europe. Undeterred by the controversies raging around Cartesianism, he was looking for a new professor to build up the university's philosophy department, and after reading a few chapters of Spinoza's work on Descartes—he seems at that point to have been unaware of the *Treatise*, or at least of its author's identity—he determined that Spinoza was his man. "You will not find elsewhere a Prince more favourably disposed to men of exceptional genius, among whom he ranks you," wrote Karl Ludwig's representative. "You will have the most extensive freedom in philosophising, which he believes you will not misuse to disturb the publicly established religion. . . . [I]f you come here, you will have the pleasure of living a life worthy of a philosopher, unless everything turns out contrary to our hope and expectation." Spinoza took the offer seriously, but the clause almost casually attached to the second of these reassurances stuck in his craw: *which he believes you will not misuse to disturb the publicly established religion.* For Spinoza, true freedom in philosophizing had always meant and would always mean the freedom to follow reason wherever it leads, even to conclusions that others find distasteful.

A month after receiving the offer, Spinoza wrote a gracious letter of refusal. Had he been interested in a public teaching position, he wrote, he could not have wished for a more appealing proposal. But, he continued, "I do not know within what limits the freedom to philosophise must be confined if I am to avoid appearing to disturb the publicly established religion. . . . So you see, most Honourable Sir, that my reluctance is not due to the hope of some better fortune, but to my love of peace, which I believe I can enjoy in some measure if I refrain from lecturing in public." Freedom to think and express his views was far more important to Spinoza than the honor, influence, and financial security of a prestigious university appointment. His quiet life at the Van der Spycks' was perfectly adequate for his purposes.

Another flattering sign of recognition came just a few months later when large parts of the country were still occupied by the foreign forces that had invaded during the Disaster Year. The city of Utrecht was the nerve center of France's occupying forces, and the man in charge, Louis de Bourbon, the prince of Condé, was one of the most powerful members of the French nobility. The prince was not only a brilliant general but a cultured patron of the arts who liked to surround himself with gifted writers and thinkers. During his stay in Utrecht, he was trying to recreate the intellectual environment that he had left behind in France. Spinoza was an obvious choice.

Spinoza accepted the prince of Condé's invitation, and in the summer of 1673, the philosopher made his way to the city of Utrecht, behind enemy lines. Unfortunately, he seems never to have actually met the prince, who had been called out of town for an unexpectedly long period of time. Nonetheless, for a brief interlude, Spinoza was able to enjoy the gracious hospitality of his French hosts as well as the stimulating company of other Dutch intellectuals. One fortunate outcome of the adventure was a much improved relationship with Lambert van Velthuysen, the prominent Cartesian

THE PRINCE OF CONDÉ: The prince was an outstanding general, a fabulously rich aristocrat, and a serious intellectual. When he was not engaged in warfare, he enjoyed the company of brilliant thinkers and writers whose work he generously supported.

Louis de Bourbon, IIe du nom, Prince de Condé, surnommé Monsieur le Prince, engraving by Robert Nanteuil, 1662. Yale University Art Gallery.

whose insulting comments about the *Treatise* had provoked one of Spinoza's rare outbursts of irritation. Although certainly not in agreement about everything, the two men gained much more respect for each other during their time together in Utrecht.

But once again, Spinoza had abandoned his habitual caution in his earnest desire to communicate with like-minded people. He was already the subject of deep mistrust, and his journey into French territory did not endear him to the people back home. A rumor began to circulate that the philosopher was a spy working in collusion with the French to destroy the Republic, and upon Spinoza's return, Van der Spyck once again had cause to worry about the safety of his tenant, his family, and his property. Spinoza reassured his landlord, at least on the second and third of these concerns. If an angry mob gathered around the Van der Spycks' door, Spinoza promised, "I'll go outside, and I'll go straight to them, even if they were to treat me the same way they treated the poor De Witts." Fortunately, Spinoza had no occasion to put his words to the test.

Spinoza would forever remain the bane of Calvinists and other traditionalists unwilling to live side by side with those who had other ways of looking at the world. But his international renown, which had reached even powerful European princes, would today earn the envy of a self-promoting celebrity with an entire public relations staff. And yet with the exception of his trip to Utrecht, Spinoza had never altered his quiet habits or ventured out of the small swath of the Republic in which he had always lived.

CHAPTER TWENTY-SIX

DISCOURAGING EVENTS

FAME CAN BE PERSONALLY AFFIRMING, BUT SPINOZA had never sought it. He had an almost eerie self-sufficiency that left him largely unconcerned about others' opinions. And fame was beginning to put heavy demands on his schedule. It did not help that he found his health getting noticeably worse. His coughing fits were longer and more frequent, and his breathing grew increasingly labored. As it became harder for him to complete the tasks he set out for himself, his time felt more and more precious.

In 1675 Spinoza finally finished writing the *Ethics*, which had preoccupied him in one way or another for almost two decades. But with True Freedom over and the *Treatise* officially banned, the prospects for publishing the new manuscript were dim. In many ways, the *Ethics* was more daring than the detested *Treatise*. The *Treatise* had only hinted at Spinoza's rejection of a traditional, transcendent God who acts freely upon the world, but the *Ethics* presented that view loudly and clearly. The God of the *Ethics* was the impersonal substance of nature, with no will, no freedom, and no concern for human beings.

Spinoza was also under close watch by religious authorities who were determined to prevent any further publication of his alarming ideas. Nonetheless, toward the end of July 1675, Spinoza resolutely made his way to Amsterdam and presented his manuscript to his trusty publisher. Rieuwertsz, undaunted as ever, was thrilled to take on the project. Up to this point, Spinoza had allowed various drafts to circulate only among his closest group of friends, who were under the strictest orders not to share them or even to talk about them with anyone else.

As it turned out, Spinoza's visit to Amsterdam coincided with a major landmark in the lives of the Portuguese Jews: the Nation had just completed the construction of a majestic new synagogue. Clearly, by 1675 the community felt sufficiently established to drop its usual concerns about attracting too much attention from the outside world. The building was imposing, and the celebration was loud. The joyous gala continued for eight days, and it seemed that all of Amsterdam, both Jewish and non-Jewish, was in attendance. The new synagogue, which still stands proudly today, was the talk of the town.

Spinoza may well have indulged his curiosity in a walk over to the old neighborhood. There the streets and faces, once so familiar, would have contrasted with an overwhelming sense of foreignness. Spinoza was now so intellectually and emotionally removed from the Jewish community that his former life there almost seemed as if it had been lived by an entirely different person.

The Nation's expansive sense of security would also have contrasted sharply with Spinoza's awareness that the authorities were closing in on him. During his stay in Amsterdam, he kept hearing rather discouraging rumors. His activities were being monitored not only by the religious establishment but also by political authorities, all of whom were poised for attack should another book by Spinoza begin to circulate. The reports were so alarming that within two weeks of handing the *Ethics* over to Rieuwertsz, Spinoza put a sudden halt to the printing process. He returned to The Hague, and there he locked his shining triumph, the masterpiece into which he had poured years of painstaking effort, into the dark drawer of his writing desk.

SYNAGOGUE DEDICATION: To celebrate Talmud Torah's newly completed building, a cantor recites prayers from the *bima*, the raised platform in the center. Community leaders holding Torah scrolls march down the left-hand aisle toward the *aron*, the imposing cabinet that houses the holy scrolls when they are not in use.

Dedication of the Synagogue of Portuguese Jews in Amsterdam by Bernard Picard, in *Cérémonies et coûtumes religieuses de tous les peuples du monde* (Amsterdam, 1724–1737). Stadsarchief Amsterdam.

The fall of 1675 must have been depressing. With no prospect of publishing the *Ethics* in the foreseeable future and with his health continuing to deteriorate, Spinoza might have wondered what he had achieved, after all, with the best of his efforts. A letter that arrived during that period only deepened the gloom. The writer was Albert Burgh, a promising young man Spinoza had taught at Van den Enden's school. Albert Burgh belonged to an extremely influential and wealthy merchant family who had entertained great hopes for his future. But on his recent travels in Italy, Burgh had undergone a religious awakening and converted to Catholicism. He had taken a vow of poverty and had completely abandoned the comfortable lifestyle in which he had been raised. He now wore only an old, ragged habit, and he walked around barefoot, even for the longest of distances in the worst of weather. His bewildered parents tried to reason with him, and when that failed to work, they cut off his allowance. He simply laughed at them and pitied their lack of understanding.

Burgh's letter, sent from Italy, was a fervent attempt to help Spinoza see the light. "The more I have admired you in the past for the penetration and acuity of your mind," wrote Burgh, "the more do I now moan and lament for you." Spinoza, according to Burgh, had allowed himself "to be entrapped and deceived by that most wretched and arrogant Prince of evil spirits," and at risk was Spinoza's peace of mind in this life and the salvation of his soul in the next life. The only way for Spinoza to save himself was to abandon his sins and his "wretched, insane way of reasoning." By the end of the letter, Burgh's tone turned sharply aggressive. He accused Spinoza of having become "foolishly proud and puffed up" by a sense of superiority as well as by the admiration of other people.

Spinoza did not respond right away. In Burgh's current state, any attempt to persuade through reason might prove fruitless or even confirm the young man in his extravagant foolishness. But Burgh's father was desperate for help, and Spinoza finally agreed to write back. Spinoza's letter displayed little of his usual levelheaded cool. "[U]nless perchance you have lost your memory together with your reason," he cuttingly told Burgh, "you will not be able to deny that in every Church there are very many honourable people who worship God with justice and charity." In Spinoza's view, the religious beliefs and rituals one adopted were beside the point, since true religion had nothing to do with Catholicism or Puritanism or Lutheranism or Judaism or any other sect. Had Burgh understood this properly, he would not have caused his family such heartache.

And then Spinoza's language became truly heated: "And do you bewail me, wretched man? And do you call my philosophy, which you have never beheld, a chimera?" Spinoza might have been willing to let Burgh, like anyone else, go his own way and adopt the specific beliefs and rituals that appealed to him personally. But Burgh had attacked reason itself, and this Spinoza could not tolerate. On the counterattack, Spinoza moved into the sneering tone that had been more characteristic of his friend Adriaan Koerbagh. Singling out the Catholic belief that Jesus's body is genuinely present in the bread of the Eucharist, Spinoza scoffed, "O youth deprived of understanding, who has bewitched you into believing that you eat, and hold in your intestines, that which is supreme and eternal?" Spinoza pointed out that Burgh's obsession with ritual stemmed from the usual source: "[Y]ou have become the slave of this Church not so much through love of God as fear of Hell, which is the single cause of superstition."

Spinoza urged Burgh to drop the fear and superstition that had led him to adopt beliefs and rituals that violated reason. Burgh claimed to be entirely convinced of the truth of his newfound faith, but Spinoza reminded him that people in faiths widely different from Catholicism had been just as convinced of the truth of their own beliefs—

even to the point of martyrdom. In a rare and moving reference to his own Jewish background, Spinoza mentioned the kind of report he must have heard as a child, living among members of the Nation who ached for news about loved ones still within the Inquisition's grasp. He wrote, "I myself know among others of a certain Judah called 'the faithful' who, in the midst of the flames when he was already believed dead, started to sing the hymn which begins, 'To Thee, O God, I commit my soul,' and so singing, died."

Reason, by contrast, could never lead people astray because conclusions based on reason are as indisputable as mathematical proofs. "I do not presume that I have found the best philosophy," Spinoza asserted, "but I know that what I understand is the true one. If you ask me how I know this, I reply that I know it in the same way that you know that the three angles of a triangle are equal to two right angles." Reason is "the true Word of God, which is in the mind and can never be distorted or corrupted."

Spinoza's letter failed to have its desired effect. Still barefoot and draped in his ragged habit, Burgh journeyed back from Italy to Amsterdam, begging for charity the entire way. His parents were entirely at their wit's end during his stay. When he left a short while later to join a Franciscan monastery in

Rome, their feelings of loss must have been partly offset by a guilty sense of relief at his departure. From Spinoza's perspective, the confrontation with Burgh had been a miniature version of the far larger war he was waging against unreason. But on the small scale as well as the large one, the attempt to combat superstition with reason had come to nothing.

Spinoza bravely carried on. A single student whose mind he had failed to reach paled in comparison to a two-decade effort locked away in a desk drawer, but even the more intense disappointment did not deter the philosopher from his work. With his customary faith that reason could not fail to triumph, he began to work on an annotated new edition of the *Theological-Political Treatise* to "remove prejudices which have been conceived against it." Spinoza's plan was to include the major objections that had arisen in response to the first edition, along with his own responses to those objections. Among the people he consulted for this new edition were Henry Oldenburg and Lambert van Velthuysen, both of whom had been scathingly critical of the original work but had become sufficiently reconciled with Spinoza himself to offer their thoughts in response.

Another project was quite different in nature. Spinoza had argued in the *Treatise* that a proper reading of the Bible requires a solid knowledge of the Hebrew language, but many of his friends, eager to follow his recommendations, lacked that knowledge. Spinoza's childhood grounding in biblical Hebrew now came in handy, and he sat down to compose a guide to Hebrew grammar.

Spinoza also began to expand upon some of the political issues that he had only touched upon in his earlier writings. His new work, the *Political Treatise*, was an attempt to address the real world, not to present an ideal accessible to only a select few. And so, while the *Ethics* presents passions as something to be overcome, the *Political Treatise* views them more neutrally:

> *I have taken great care not to deride, bewail, or execrate human actions, but to understand them. So I have regarded human emotions such as love, hatred, anger, envy, pride, pity, and other agitations of the mind not as vices of human nature but as properties pertaining to it in the same way as heat, cold, storm, thunder, and such pertain to the nature of the atmosphere.*

It is with the same realistic spirit that Spinoza discusses various forms of government. Although he emphasizes, as he had already done in the

Theological-Political Treatise, that democracy is the ideal form of government, he recognizes that many countries, for a variety of reasons, cannot or will not transform themselves into democracies. Spinoza therefore provides many concrete suggestions for making other forms of government the very best that they can be—in effect, to make them as democratic as possible under the existing arrangements.

Unfortunately, Spinoza did not survive long enough to finish the *Political Treatise,* and his work was interrupted just as he had begun to present the specific political arrangements of his ideal democracy. And, just as unfortunately, the last point he made was that women could not possibly be full participants in a democracy, either as voters or as elected officials, because of their inherent inferiority to men. Spinoza was in most ways so far ahead of his time that it is easy to forget that such a view of women was entirely accepted in his day and age.

Far more fortunate is the lasting inspiration of Spinoza's vision. A democracy firmly committed to freedom of thought and expression, he argued, is the form of government best suited to the natural equality and natural strivings of human beings. Since each of us has been endowed with reason, it makes no sense, either logically or ethically, for us to let others do our thinking for us—whether those others be political figures or religious authorities. Spinoza's unwavering insistence on this point, so contested in his own day even in the most tolerant country in all of Europe, has indeed changed the way we see the world. Freedom of thought and expression have become axiomatic features of modern democracies.

CHAPTER TWENTY-SEVEN

PERSONAL
ENCOUNTERS

SPINOZA'S HEALTH DETERIORATED RAPIDLY DURING
the winter of 1676–1677. He frequently spat up
blood, and he often felt overcome by a leaden
weariness. Although he tried to keep his suffering
to himself, his discomfort was obvious from his
labored breathing and persistent coughing. When
his condition seemed especially poor, his landlady,
Ida van der Spyck, made it a point to bring him
warm and soothing broths.

One day she lingered longer than necessary in
Spinoza's room. On the streets of The Hague, she
could hardly have avoided the wild rumors about
her famous tenant, and on more than one occasion,
she must have found herself the subject of angry
comments and questions. How could she, a good
Christian woman, house such a wicked man, the
devil himself, under her roof? Wasn't she afraid for

the welfare of her soul, not to mention the tender souls of the little children she was exposing to such an evil influence?

But Ida van der Spyck could not think of Spinoza as a bad man, despite everything that people said about him. For one thing, he had a lovely way with her children. Far from being a negative influence on them, he gently encouraged them to behave politely and respect their elders, and there was something about him—his soft-spoken earnestness, perhaps, which his visitors always found so compelling—that made her children do as he said. And when anyone in the household fell ill, he made it his business to offer whatever comfort he could. She and her husband genuinely enjoyed his company when he joined them, equipped with his favorite pipe, for an evening chat.

The question she had for Spinoza had been weighing on her for a long time, and she finally brought herself to ask it. Could she be saved in the religion she professed?

Spinoza did not hesitate in his response. "Your religion is good," he assured his landlady, whom he knew to be an honest and sincere woman, devoted to those she loved. "You need not look for another one, nor doubt that you may be saved in it, provided that while you apply yourself to piety, you live at the same time a peaceful and tranquil life."

Spinoza accepted the idea that some people would always need the outward, more superstitious forms of traditional religion, but he never wavered from his view that the highest form of blessedness is available only to those who pursue the life of pure reason. In the winter of 1676, when the dreariness and cold were weighing heavily upon him, Spinoza enjoyed a visit from a man who was earnestly pursuing that life and was quite likely the most intelligent person he had ever met. Although this man eventually came to conclusions that were radically different from Spinoza's, he was destined to be counted, along with Descartes and Spinoza himself, as one of the three greatest philosophers of the century.

Spinoza's visitor was a young German man named Gottfried Wilhelm Leibniz. Leibniz was about as different from Spinoza as a person could possibly be. Leibniz had the highest opinion of himself, which he was happy to share with anyone who would listen—as well as with anyone not particularly interested in listening. He loved wealth and power, and since he was not independently wealthy or powerful, he spent his life trying to stay in the good graces of people who were. He mingled among the rich and stylish set wherever he lived, and he did his best to keep up. He dressed well, dined well, enjoyed fashionable pursuits, and spent a lot of time flattering the people on whom he depended. Often the effort to flatter meant adjusting his views—or at least the views he expressed publicly—to meet the needs of his listeners.

As it turned out, Leibniz had done a bit of that adjusting regarding Spinoza himself. Leibniz had once been the student of Jakob Thomasius, the professor responsible for the very first published attack on the *Theological-Political Treatise*. Upon

GOTTFRIED WILHELM LEIBNIZ: This brilliant thinker once wrote to a friend, "I can't tell you how distracted a life I am leading . . . I have so much that is new in mathematics, so many thoughts in philosophy, so numerous literary observations of other kinds, which I do not wish to lose, that I am often at a loss what to do first" (Stewart, 256). No such disorder characterized Leibniz's physical appearance. In this portrait, his extravagant wig and clothing are a far cry from Spinoza's quiet modesty.

Portrait from John Theodore Merz's *Leibniz* (Edinburgh: Blackwood, 1884). University Library, University of Michigan.

seeing his former teacher's abrasive review, Leibniz
sent him a congratulatory note, affirming that
Thomasius had treated the "intolerably impudent"
work "as it deserves." At that point, Leibniz probably
did not know who had written the *Treatise*. A few
months later, when Leibniz certainly did know the
secret, he persisted in the same vein. In a letter to
a different correspondent, he expressed his sorrow
that "such a learned man has, as it seems, sunk
so low." And yet less than half a year later, Leibniz
wrote Spinoza a flattering letter whose goal was to
initiate an intellectual exchange of ideas by mail. In
the letter, the slippery Leibniz praised Spinoza as a
"celebrated doctor and profound philosopher."

More recently, Leibniz had been eagerly trying
to get his hands on a draft of the as-yet unpublished
Ethics. Like many others, Leibniz had heard rumors
that Spinoza had written and was seeking to publish
something even more daring than the *Theological-
Political Treatise*. But Leibniz had also heard about
the work more reliably and directly through one of
the new members of Spinoza's inner circle from
Amsterdam, a young man who had his own copy of
the manuscript and wanted permission to show it
to Leibniz. Spinoza refused. "As far as I can judge
from his letter," Spinoza wrote regarding Leibniz,
"he seemed to me a person of liberal mind and well
versed in every science. Still, I think it imprudent

to entrust my writings to him so hastily." Perhaps Spinoza, through letters now lost, sensed something of Leibniz's compulsive opportunism.

In any case, five years after receiving Leibniz's first letter, Spinoza welcomed the young German man into his humble lodgings at the Van der Spycks'. It must have been a fascinating study of opposites. With perfectly coiffed wig, elegant hosiery, mannerly bearing, and polished speech, Leibniz made his graceful way into the single, unpretentious chamber that served his host as combined bedroom, living room, dining room, and workroom—a far cry from the fine salons of Europe to which Leibniz was accustomed. Spinoza, wearing neat but obviously well-worn clothing in the simplest of styles, could offer his sophisticated visitor little more comfort than a hard wooden chair pulled up to a bare wooden table.

But there was no disparity in the power of the two men's minds. Leibniz was a brilliant man, one of the greatest geniuses of the seventeenth century and arguably of all time. His remarkable abilities shone in just about every intellectual field that one can name, from mathematics to science to philosophy to history to law—and the list continues. In the eighteenth century, Denis Diderot, a brilliant thinker in his own right, expressed utter awe at the man's abilities, despite being no great fan of some of

Leibniz's ideas. "When one . . . compares one's own small talents with those of a Leibniz," Diderot wrote, "one is tempted to throw away one's books and go die peacefully in the depths of some dark corner."

Leibniz and Spinoza shared a profound awareness of the entirely new world that had been ushered in by Cartesianism and the new science. If the world was really a machine operating according to impersonal and unchangeable laws, the old comforts had run their course. Gone were the old certainties about God, the reassuring rule books for proper behavior, the promised rewards for a life well lived, the guarantee that good ultimately triumphs over evil. People had no choice but to find a new path through the chillingly barren landscape in which they now found themselves.

Spinoza responded by fully embracing the new reality. No, God is not a loving father who makes everything all right. No, there is no authoritative set of rules by which we must live. No, there is no reward in heaven for leading a moral life. No, there is no guarantee that good ultimately triumphs. In fact, there is no evidence that "good" names an objective reality in the first place. But none of this is cause for despair. The new world, stripped of all its old comforts, is a call to action. If we cannot find external signs that all is well in the world, we must find that reassurance within ourselves. If the rule books we once used no longer seem authoritative, we must learn to define our own course. If we cannot expect to earn prizes for morality, we must consider the moral life a reward in itself. If we cannot expect good to triumph over evil, we must understand that we are simply one little part of an all-embracing, intricately interconnected system—call it what you will: substance, nature, God—with a grandiose beauty of its own. And reason, the awesome power that lies within each of us, is the means by which we can achieve each of these goals—in other words, the means by which we achieve blessedness.

Leibniz's response was quite different. He was not convinced that a new foundation, independent of the old religious assumptions, would be strong enough to support a system of morality, a sense of human worth, and a life of fulfillment. He also worried that when the harsh light of reason illuminates absolutely everything, there is no room left for mystery or spirit—for any sense that there exists, somewhere in the great beyond, something bigger and better than we can ever be ourselves, and that that something invests our lives with meaning. And yet, unlike Spinoza's Calvinist foes, Leibniz was too committed to reason simply to dismiss the mechanistic, rule-governed view of the universe. Instead, he attempted to bridge the old and new worlds. Much of his philosophy is an attempt to ground the old religious certainties in the uncharted landscape of the new science and its mathematical truth.

Leibniz, for instance, could not accept Spinoza's identification of God with the substance of nature. For Leibniz, such a God is not a God at all. A God worthy of the name cannot be bound by the necessity of nature but must have the freedom to exercise intellect, make choices, and demonstrate goodness. But how could a completely rule-driven universe coexist with a God who transcended those rules? Long after his visit to The Hague, Leibniz eventually found his answer to this question; he simply needed to push God's arena of freedom back a step. God's freedom finds expression not in the individual things of our world but in the fact of our world altogether. According to Leibniz, we occupy only one of an infinite number of possible worlds, and each of those possible worlds comes with its own distinctive set of natural laws. God freely chose to create the particular world that we inhabit because, with perfect intellect and infinite goodness, God recognized it as the "best of all possible worlds." Once our particular world was created, its distinctive set of natural laws came into play, and now everything that happens does indeed happen necessarily.

LETTER TO LEIBNIZ: The signature "B. d'espinoza" appears at the end of this letter. In the postscript, Spinoza expresses his misgivings about relying on an "ordinary letter-carrier" and asks Leibniz if he has any reliable acquaintances in The Hague "so that our letters can be dispatched more conveniently and safely." Spinoza is obviously worried that their correspondence will fall into the wrong hands.

Spinoza's letter to Leibniz (Letter 46), November 9, 1671. Hannover: Gottfried Wilhem Leibniz Library, Lower Saxony State Library, Lbr. 886.

Leibniz's system also rejected Spinoza's reduction of humankind to just another bit of nature buffeted about by impersonal, natural forces. For Leibniz, the human being is indeed what Spinoza dismissed in the *Ethics* as "a kingdom within a kingdom," the occupant of a special, exalted place within God's creation. Human will is free, and the human soul continues to exist after the body's death. To maintain these ideas, Leibniz needed to reject Spinoza's notion of a single substance. Through a complex but internally logical chain of reasoning, Leibniz arrived at the idea that reality consists of an infinite number of substances. In other words, although nature operates like a machine, not everything in the world can be collapsed into the same set of mechanical rules.

Leibniz and Spinoza must have shared some fascinating conversations. Although Leibniz, with his characteristic slipperiness, later tried to play down and even deny his connection with Spinoza, it is clear that the encounter made a deep impression on him. Thirty years after his trip to The Hague, Leibniz wrote a philosophical dialogue in which one of his characters voices words that Leibniz might have uttered about himself: "You know that I once went a little too far, and began to lean to the side of the Spinozists." And although Leibniz, like so many others of his day, ended up using the name

"Spinoza" as shorthand for godless, evil thinking that undermined religion, respect for authority, and morality, he could not help but recognize Spinoza's own goodness. Spinoza's motives, Leibniz acknowledged, were just as worthy as he considered his own to be. Spinoza was the type of man who "says what he believes to be true" and firmly believes "that he is serving all humankind in delivering it from ill-founded superstitions." Furthermore, Leibniz wrote, Spinoza was one of the great thinkers who "led entirely exemplary lives" and served as an example of "people of an excellent nature who would never be led by [their] doctrines to do anything unworthy of themselves."

We have no record of what Leibniz and Spinoza said to each other during the winter of 1676, but more than three centuries later, our world continues to be shaken by the same conflict between faith and reason that preoccupied those two men. Debates continue to rage about the existence of God, the authority of the Bible, the objectivity of good and evil, the freedom of human action, the idea of the soul—almost all the major topics we can imagine the two philosophers discussing. And our responses today echo what the two men must have said back then. There are the Spinozas among us who have simply walked away from the old neighborhood and never looked back. They have left behind the old traditions like so much rubble, and they have set out to build everything afresh, unflinchingly, on a new foundation of pure reason. And there are the Leibnizes who find that the pristine structure of reason is a very cold place to live. They long for something transcendent, for the comfort that everything matters and makes sense, for the feeling that we are nurtured and loved by something greater than we are ourselves. Even in the new world that we are constructing afresh, the Leibnizes insist on the value of the trusty old building blocks.

Interactions between the Leibnizes and the Spinozas of our day are often venomous and contemptuous. But perhaps we can imagine both sides still sitting at a bare wooden table in a modest room in The Hague, listening respectfully to each other's ideas, recognizing that they confront the same set of challenges, and appreciating their shared commitment to thinking their way to truth.

CHAPTER TWENTY-EIGHT

DEATH AND ITS AFTERMATH

SPINOZA LIVED HIS PHILOSOPHY THROUGH AND through. In the *Ethics* he had written that a "free man thinks of death least of all things, and his wisdom is a meditation of life, not of death." Despite his rapidly deteriorating health, Spinoza spent very little time worrying about the future.

According to an early biographer who spoke to the Van der Spycks about their famous tenant, Spinoza "would say sometimes to the other lodgers that he was like the serpent that forms a circle with its tail in its mouth, meaning that he had nothing left of what he might have earned during the year." Spinoza apparently had more to say on the topic: "He added that it was not his intention to save any more money than what would be necessary for him to have a decent burial. Just as his parents had left him nothing, so too his relatives and heirs should not expect to profit much by his death." In keeping with this conviction, Spinoza did not bother to prepare a will.

Nonetheless, Spinoza realized that it would be foolish to neglect at least one practical arrangement. There was still the question of his philosophical masterpiece locked away in his desk drawer— the *Ethics*, whose publication he had regretfully halted almost a year and a half earlier. And now, locked away with the *Ethics*, were his more recent manuscripts, along with his considerable personal correspondence. Spinoza believed just as urgently as ever in his message to the world, and whether he lived or died, he wanted his work to be published. For this to happen, it was absolutely essential that his manuscripts not fall into the wrong hands. There were plenty of watchful people out there with every interest in consigning Spinoza and his ideas to eternal oblivion.

And so the one preparation that Spinoza made in the event of his untimely death concerned his writings. He gave Hendrik van der Spyck the strictest of instructions. Upon his death, his entire desk, still locked, was to be shipped directly to Jan Rieuwertsz in Amsterdam. Spinoza's trustworthy and intrepid publisher would know exactly what to do with the precious manuscripts the desk contained.

One wintry Saturday, the Van der Spycks went to church, as was their custom, for afternoon services. When they returned home at about four o'clock, Spinoza joined them in their sitting room, filled his pipe, sat back, and asked about the sermon they had just heard. But despite his adherence to his usual routine, Spinoza was not feeling particularly well, and a short time later he retired to his room for the night. The next morning, before his landlords left once again for church, Spinoza informed them that he had sent for a doctor from Amsterdam. The doctor had requested that the Van der Spycks prepare a chicken broth for Spinoza to eat later in the day.

The Van der Spycks readily complied with the doctor's request, and upon their return from church, Spinoza ate the broth they had prepared for him. Since he ate with a good appetite and was already in the care of the doctor from Amsterdam, the Van der Spycks had no particular cause for concern and went back to church for afternoon services. But when they returned home, they discovered that Spinoza had passed away peacefully and in his own bed, attended by the doctor, during their absence. It was February 21, 1677. Spinoza was only forty-four years old.

Hendrik van der Spyck made arrangements for the burial, which took place four days later at the Nieuwe Kerk in the center of town. Enough mourners gathered to fill the six coaches that followed the wagon carrying the coffin. After the funeral, following Dutch custom, the mourners returned to the Van der Spyck house to share some wine and talk about the deceased.

It is unclear whether anyone from the Jewish community attended the funeral. What is certain, however, is that a couple of weeks later, after more than twenty years of being completely out of touch, Spinoza's sister Rebecca identified herself and a nephew as the philosopher's sole legitimate heirs. Rebecca authorized Van der Spyck to make a list of whatever possessions Spinoza had left behind, and Van der Spyck promptly did so—but only after having sent the locked desk, its precious contents intact, to Rieuwertsz.

It turned out that Spinoza had indeed lived "like the serpent that forms a circle with its tail in its mouth," with nothing to bequeath to his relatives. He had left behind some clothing, furniture, and books, but it was not clear that their sale would generate enough money to cover what he still owed to the pharmacist, the barber, and other local tradespeople. Additionally, Van der Spyck was owed money for the funeral expenses as well as for Spinoza's room and board. Concerned that she would end up losing money rather than gaining any, Rebecca quickly withdrew the family's claim to the inheritance. As it turned out, the sale of Spinoza's possessions covered his assorted bills but not the amount due to Van der Spyck. That final obligation was settled by the family of Simon Joosten de Vries, ever faithful to the friendship that had existed between the two men.

Of course, Spinoza had left behind some absolutely priceless possessions. Those were now in the care of Rieuwertsz, who quietly convened the members of Spinoza's Amsterdam circle, including Lodewijk Meyer, Jarig Jellesz, and other long-standing friends, to discuss how to proceed. The group, knowing full well that it was taking a tremendous risk, chose the most daring of strategies: to publish all of Spinoza's works as quickly as possible in both Latin and Dutch. In the space of just a few months, Spinoza's dedicated and energetic friends edited his manuscripts, collected and sorted through his private letters, refined his Latin, translated his Latin into Dutch (and, less frequently, his Dutch into Latin), compiled an index, and wrote a general introduction to the entire anthology. All the while, the collaborators kept their work an absolute secret. Rumors about the *Ethics* were still swirling around, and Spinoza's enemies were determined to prevent its publication. The race was on.

It was actually not the local Dutch but the faraway leaders of the Catholic Church who put together the most organized campaign to stop any further publication of Spinoza's work. Albert Burgh, the young man who had experienced a Catholic awakening, seems to have informed the Inquisition in Rome that at least one new soul-destroying manuscript by his former teacher was on its way to the general public. In response, the Inquisition immediately appointed one of Amsterdam's Catholic priests to investigate. The priest assembled a task force remarkable for its interfaith composition— himself, a Protestant preacher-in-training, and a rabbi—which reflected just how deep a threat Spinoza's ideas posed to any and all religions.

The rabbi was apparently the one to discover, through Spinoza's sister and nephew, the critical information: the documents were in the possession of Rieuwertsz. The priest immediately paid the publisher a visit. But Rieuwertsz's poker face must have been astonishingly convincing. "This bookseller assured me," the priest reported back to the Inquisition, "there are no manuscripts among Spinoza's legacy apart from that of *De Principiis Philosophiae Cartesianae* [*Descartes's Principles of Philosophy*] and that no other work of Spinoza's has been published apart from the *Tractatus Theologico-Politicus* [*Theological-Political Treatise*]."

B. D. S.

OPERA

POSTHUMA,

Quorum series post Præfationem exhibetur.

cIɔ Iɔ c LXXVII.

OPERA POSTHUMA: When Spinoza's friends anthologized his philosophical works after his death, they provided no information about the publisher or place of publication. "B.D.S." reveals the author's identity, but Spinoza was already beyond the reach of his detractors.

From *B. d. S. Opera posthuma . . .* 1677. Rare Book and Manuscript Library, Columbia University in the City of New York.

Spinoza did not live to see it, but through the devoted efforts of his friends, he had finally won. In January 1678, less than a year after his death, his entire collection of philosophical writings, including his precious *Ethics*, began reaching the bookstores. The collection was called the *Opera Posthuma*— meaning "the works [published] after death." The author was identified as only B.d.S., but by that point the quiet philosopher had made enough of a mark for everyone to know exactly who that was.

Epilogue

IT IS IMPOSSIBLE TO OVERESTIMATE THE EFFECT
that Spinoza has had on our world. His ideas have
found their way into contemporary thinking about
practically all the areas he touched, including
democratic theory, freedom of thought and
expression, the conflict between faith and science,
the authorship of the Bible, the relationship
between reason and the emotions, and the freedom
or necessity of human action. And it is impossible
not to see the relevance of his views to modern
questions. What should be taught in our schools—
the biblical story of creation, the scientific account
of the universe's origins, or both? Is it legitimate
to insist on a particular view of marriage because
it is the view presented by the Bible? Does a city
government have the right to put on display the
symbols of a specific religion's holidays? Should

a criminal whose moral growth was stunted by a vicious upbringing be held legally responsible for his or her actions?

Spinoza's ideas often took a roundabout route on their way to us. The *Opera Posthuma*, not surprisingly, made an immediate, notorious impact, and in no time at all, the Dutch Republic banned not only Spinoza's own writings but the works of all other writers who dared to restate or rework his ideas. Other European countries soon followed suit. Individuals known to spread aspects of Spinoza's philosophy, whether in writing or in speech, could find themselves hounded out of their jobs and communities by a merciless public. For at least a hundred years, and even longer in some circles, "Spinoza" was a dirty word.

But Spinozism, even from the very beginning, was an underground movement, and it grew more and more powerful over time. Spinozist circles, much like the early one Spinoza had himself led in Amsterdam, multiplied throughout Europe, and authors, publishers, and booksellers—often at great personal sacrifice—found ways to spread the philosopher's ideas while eluding ever-watchful authorities. One person deeply influenced by Spinoza's ideas was the English political thinker John Locke, who in turn influenced the founding fathers of American democracy—most notably

Thomas Jefferson, the author of the Declaration of Independence, who had a copy of the *Opera Posthuma* in his personal library. By the 1800s, prominent writers and thinkers, such as Johann Wolfgang von Goethe in Germany and George Eliot in England, were no longer afraid to acknowledge openly their indebtedness to Spinoza. By the twentieth century, many people felt no particular shock or disgust upon hearing Albert Einstein's famous response to the question of whether or not he believed in God: "I believe in Spinoza's God, who reveals Himself in the orderly harmony of what exists, not in a God who concerns Himself with fates and actions of human beings."

Spinoza's enemies were certainly right to fear his impact on authority, tradition, and religion, which have never quite recovered from the harsh and systematic scrutiny to which he subjected them. But today, vast numbers of people welcome this kind of scrutiny. Most of us agree that mature individuals who take themselves seriously must learn to use their own minds. Our deepest convictions must grow out of more than the accident of being born into a particular family or into a particular culture. Relying on such accidents to shape our ideas violates the faculty of reason that is our greatest endowment. Thinking our way to our own conclusions is more than a rational option: it is the only responsible course available to us.

This attitude and the freedom to act upon it are perhaps the greatest legacy that Spinoza has left us. And it is completely characteristic of Spinoza that he left us this legacy not only in his philosophical works but also in the way he lived his life. Spinoza refused to accept ideas simply because he had inherited them. He never wavered from his view that the greatest expression of our humanity is our faculty of reason and that we violate our own dignity when we fail to use our own minds. Spinoza's convictions took him into uncharted and dangerous territory, where he stood almost entirely alone. If that territory no longer seems quite so unfamiliar, threatening, or isolating, it is because of our tremendous debt to this quietly brave man who insisted on his own way to blessedness.

Notes

PART ONE: *A Jew in Amsterdam*

Prologue

3. *The crowd was somber:* My imaginative reconstruction of the scene is based on Lucas's grim depiction of excommunication (Wolf, 52–53) and on information under the entry "*Herem*" in the *Encyclopaedia Judaica*.

4. *"Cursed be he by day":* Nadler, *Spinoza: A Life*, 120.

Chapter 1: Persecution in Spain and Portugal

9. *their major targets were Jews:* Spanish Muslims, or Moors, also suffered. Ferdinand and Isabella initially allowed Moors to practice their religion. The royal couple hoped to avoid local revolts as well as retaliations against Christians in Islamic lands, and church leaders hoped that with gentle persuasion, the Moors would embrace Christianity. Within seven years, however, fanatical Church officials had gained the upper hand, and they instituted mass conversions and the burning of Islamic texts. The armed revolt that followed gave Christian leaders an excuse to withdraw the privileges that Muslims had enjoyed. Over the next few decades, Moors throughout Spain faced the choice of baptism or exile. Most chose baptism and began to live a perilous double life like that of the crypto-Jews. Ultimately, on April 4, 1609, King Philip III signed an edict of expulsion for the Moors. He invoked the precedent of the Jewish expulsion more than a century earlier.

12. *having a chimney . . . buying lots of vegetables . . . shopping at a butcher shop:* Ben-Sasson, 588–89.

13. *huge numbers of Jews refused to compromise their faith:* I have intentionally left out specific numbers because they are the subject of much debate. Henry Kamen discusses the issue at length in "The Mediterranean and the Expulsion of Spanish Jews in 1492," *Past and Present* 119 (1988), 30–55. Kamen's estimate, at 40,000 or 50,000, is significantly lower than the more commonly accepted numbers, which range from about 150,000 to 400,000.

13. *officially no Jews remaining:* The major events I relate in this chapter occurred over five hundred years ago, but their impact endures. On March 12, 2000, Pope John Paul II issued a sweeping apology for two millennia of cruelty by people of the Church against followers of other religions, and in 2012, Spain decided to offer citizenship to the descendants of Jews expelled in 1492—people who, despite centuries of living in other lands, are still collectively known as "Sephardic Jews" after the Hebrew word for Spain, "Sepharad." Additionally, numerous individuals with Christian backgrounds have suddenly realized that unusual family traditions, such as lighting candles in the basement on Friday evenings, link them to crypto-Jewish ancestors. Doreen Carvajal discusses such an experience in *The Forgetting River: A Modern Tale of Survival, Identity, and the Inquisition* (Riverhead Books, 2012).

Chapter 2: The Dutch Promised Land

17. *"In every generation":* This text, along with the italicized words at the end of the chapter, is my own translation of a Hebrew passage that has been part of the traditional Passover seder for well over 1,800 years. As a child, Bento would have undoubtedly heard these words at his family's table, and I find it noteworthy that he possessed a Haggadah, a guidebook to the seder, in his personal library at the time of his death

(Freudenthal, 160). I rely on my imagination when I depict Bento drawing a parallel between the Israelites' escape from Egypt to the Promised Land and his family's escape from Iberia to the Dutch Republic, but I draw on a rich tradition of persecuted people finding inspiration in the story of the Exodus. Slaves of African descent in America composed beautiful spirituals linking their own experiences to those of the ancient Hebrew slaves, and many of the Holocaust survivors among whom I was raised saw in the seder their own delivery from annihilation.

18. *their stories already had a magical, mythlike quality:* My retelling of these stories is based on Nadler, *Spinoza: A Life*, 5–7, and Roth, *Spinoza*, 239–42.

19. *England, a land where Jews had not been allowed to live for hundreds of years:* King Edward I of England had expelled all Jews from his country in 1290, and it was not until 1657 that Oliver Cromwell—influenced in part by the arguments of a rabbi from Amsterdam—officially permitted their return.

Chapter 3: Jewish Life in Amsterdam

26. *The Jews of Amsterdam were not forced to live in a ghetto:* In their freedom to live where they pleased, the Jews of Amsterdam enjoyed a privilege denied to their co-religionists in many other cities. The first ghetto was established in the early 1500s in Venice, where Jews were forced to live in a small, gated area that was carefully watched by guards. Although Jews could enter the rest of the city during the day, they were expected to return to their enclosed area by sunset and were not allowed to leave again until the following dawn. This arrangement lasted almost three centuries. The Venetians came to call the Jewish neighborhood the "ghèto," which might have referred to the metal foundry that had once existed on the site, and the term eventually entered the English language as the word "ghetto."

29. *a square island called Vlooienburg:* The island no longer exists. In 1882, the Houtgracht was filled in to form the

Waterlooplein, a commercial square that now houses a popular flea market.

32. *"Dutch Jerusalem"*: Roth, 251.

33. *the envy of much older and more established Jewish communities*: Much of our information about Amsterdam's Jewish school system comes from members of other Jewish communities. The source of my description is Nadler, *Spinoza: A Life*, 61–65.

38. *"All the earth belongs to the Holy One"*: M. Rosenbaum and A.M. Silbermann, trans., *Pentateuch with Targum Onkelos, Haphtaroth and Prayers for Sabbath and Rashi's Commentary*, vol. 1, Genesis (London: Shapiro, Valentine & Co., 1946), 2. Rashi's position as the preeminent biblical commentator had been well established for several centuries before Bento began his studies at Talmud Torah, and today, almost a millennium after his birth, Rashi still holds that position among traditional Jews. It is hardly worth debating whether Bento was familiar with Rashi's famous first comment on the Book of Genesis. More speculative is my suggestion that Bento was enthralled by a sense of belonging to a special fellowship. But he would certainly have encountered traditional texts that presented Jews as the Chosen People—after all, the Torah itself does this—and it seems likely enough that a young child would find the idea alluring.

40. *to collect some money that was owed by an old woman*: Lucas is our source for this story (Wolf, 67–68). It is difficult to know just what to make of it. On the one hand, Lucas knew Spinoza as an adult, and it is possible that the biographer heard the story firsthand. On the other hand, Lucas wanted his readers to share his own admiration for Spinoza, and the story has the suspicious feel of hero worship—much like the "I cannot tell a lie" legends associated with George Washington. Perhaps all we can say for sure is that the personality traits that the young Bento reveals in the story—his unshakable self-confidence, sharp intelligence, and canny understanding of personality types—ring true for the adult that he eventually became.

Chapter 4: Beyond the Jewish Neighborhood

43. *a much larger world beyond the Nation:* I have relied primarily on Schama and Willis in my presentation of Amsterdam in this chapter.

54. *really a game of hot potato:* Nadler, *Spinoza: A Life*, 51.

Chapter 5: Questions and Potential Consequences

61. *he began to question the familiar certainties of his life:* The truth is that we know very little about Bento's thoughts prior to his break with the Jewish community. I have relied on the skeletal account provided by Lucas (Wolf, 42–43)—essentially, little more than the picture of a young man quietly dissatisfied with his teachers' answers and jotting down his concerns for later reflection. I drew on the adult Spinoza's thoughts in the *Theological-Political Treatise* to imagine the specific issues that might have troubled him as a teenager.

64. *"The whole Torah was given us through Moses our Teacher":* Twersky, 420. I have taken these words from the twelfth-century scholar Maimonides, who is regarded as one of the greatest Jewish thinkers of all time. Because of his Spanish origins, he was especially beloved among Jews of Iberian descent, and Bento's teachers would have been thoroughly familiar with Maimonides's famous formulation of Jewish belief, the "Thirteen Principles of Faith." The quotation I put into the mouth of Bento's teacher comes from the Eighth Principle.

69. *and lashed him thirty-nine times:* The Torah authorizes a maximum of forty lashes, but the rabbis, worried about violations that might result from miscounting, set the maximum at thirty-nine. The thirty-nine times that da Costa was whipped, then, pointedly demonstrated the community's adherence to the rabbinic tradition that he had so emphatically rejected.

Chapter 6: Doubting the Immortality of the Soul

71. *well on his way to da Costa's rejection of the soul's immortality:* In Spinoza's *Heresy: Immortality and the Jewish Mind*, Nadler argues that this issue, more than any other, triggered Spinoza's excommunication.

Chapter 7: The Many Forces of Intolerance

86. *"Plainly, God desires them to live somewhere":* Nadler, *Spinoza: A Life*, 11.

86. *Community officials made every effort:* Information on how the Nation governed itself is available in Nadler, *Spinoza: A Life*, 18–19 and 37–39.

Chapter 8: The Frustrated Merchant

92. *"the hollowness and futility" . . . "a true good":* Treatise on the Emendation of the Intellect *(Spinoza: Complete Works, 3).*

Chapter 9: More Attempts at Jewish Answers

98. *Maimonides was a rationalist:* Maimonides spared no words for what he viewed as the superstition of ignoramuses. In his introduction to *The Guide of the Perplexed*, his major philosophical work, he referred frequently to the "vulgar" masses and anticipated their objections to his treatise: "those who are confused and whose brains have been polluted by false opinions and misleading ways deemed by them to be true sciences, and who hold themselves to be men of speculation without having any knowledge of anything that can truly be called science, those will flee from many of its chapters" (Moses Maimonides, *The Guide of the Perplexed*, vol. 1, Shlomo Pines, trans. [Chicago and London: University of Chicago Press, 1963], 16). Maimonides was right to predict opposition. Since mainstream Judaism included a great deal of what Maimonides disparaged, his views fed into centuries of heated disputes that are now collectively known as the Maimonidean Controversy.

101. *As he sifted through Maimonides's views:* In chapters 7 and 15 of the *Theological-Political Treatise (Spinoza: Complete Works,* 456–71; 520–26), Spinoza directly addresses Maimonides's approaches to biblical interpretation and prophecy. I do not know of a source in which Spinoza writes directly about Maimonides's views about God, but their discussions on the subject are poles apart. For a look at Maimonides's transcendental understanding of God, it is worth reading the first chapter of *Yesodei ha-Torah* ("The Basic Principles of the Torah"), which opens Maimonides's monumental presentation of Jewish law, the *Mishneh Torah* (Twersky, 43–45). Spinoza presents his very different view of God in a language and format that make for notoriously difficult reading, but the place to look is Part I of the *Ethics (Spinoza: Complete Works,* 217–43).

Chapter 10: Exploring the Wider World

103. *Beyond the basics, individuals could believe practice, and interpret the Bible as they chose:* The Collegiants were the heirs of a religious tradition that had been changed forever by the technology of printing. Just as important as Johannes Gutenberg's movable type, which replaced the laborious work of scribes, were the later and lesser-known innovations of Aldus Manutius: compact fonts and page sizes that made books portable and affordable. The growing availability of printed texts encouraged literacy, and one result was that the Bible could no longer remain the exclusive domain of religious professionals who provided authorized interpretations. Eventually, the ability of a wider public to read and think independently about the Bible helped the Protestant Reformation take hold in the sixteenth century.

104. *Bento was not interested in becoming a Christian:* There has long existed a popular belief that Spinoza, at some point in his life, converted to Christianity. Supposed evidence of this conversion consists not only in Spinoza's close relationship with the Collegiants but also in his burial in a Christian cemetery at the Nieuwe Kerk (New Church) of The

Hague. Nonetheless, the idea that Spinoza became a Christian is completely false.

104. *some very impressive bookstores:* In seventeenth-century bookstores, the store owner and his small group of workers not only sold books but often took care of all the tasks involved in producing books—evaluating and editing manuscripts; designing, typesetting, printing, and binding volumes; and marketing the finished product. In modern terms, such bookstores were really miniature publishing companies.

104. *Latin had been the dominant language:* After the fall of the Roman Empire, Latin survived mainly because it was adopted by the Catholic Church, which was responsible for most of the scholarship of the Middle Ages. Even once the Protestant Reformation had loosened Catholicism's hold on Europe, Latin maintained its preeminence. Most scholarly texts had already been written in that language, which also simplified international communication among scholars.

108. *and had written a play:* Philosopher and novelist Rebecca Goldstein humorously notes that *Lusty Heart*, the title of Van den Enden's play, "about sums up the playwright" (Goldstein, 213). Not surprisingly, civic authorities found the work objectionable and banned its production. According to Colerus, the wily Van den Enden "sowed in the spirits of the young men"—presumably including Spinoza—"the first seeds of atheism." The biographer insists that this accusation is "a fact that I could prove if there were a need to do so, through the testimony of several honest gentlemen who are still alive" (Colerus, 3–4).

108. *Clara Maria even became a teacher at his school:* Colerus praises Clara Maria for her "great deal of spirit, of ability, and of joviality" and reports that the young woman had "mastered the Latin tongue so perfectly, along with music, that she was capable of instructing her father's students in his absence." But Colerus adds the rather sour comment that she was "neither of the most beautiful nor of the best-formed" (Colerus, 4). Even if Clara Maria was not especially attractive, the

comment—or at least Colerus's decision to include it—
seems to reflect an assumption that there is something
unflattering about an educated and accomplished
woman.

Chapter 11: The Suspected Heretic

111. *No one really knows exactly what set off the alarm:*
The only clues from the Nation's records appear
in the public declaration made at Spinoza's
excommunication: communal leaders had "long
known" of Spinoza's "evil opinions and acts," and the
young man is accused of "evil ways," "wicked ways,"
"abominable heresies which he practiced and taught,"
and "monstrous deeds" (Nadler, *Spinoza: A Life*, 120).

113. *the nature of God, the authorship and authority of the
Bible, and the immortality of the soul:* The source
for these three categories is a report submitted to
the Spanish Inquisition in 1659 by the Catholic
monk Tomas Solano y Robles and his companion
Captain Miguel Perez de Maltranilla. Eager to gather
information about Amsterdam's Jewish community,
these two men met with the recently excommunicated
Spinoza and Prado. According to Brother Tomas, "it
seemed to them that the said law was not true and that
souls died with their bodies and that there is no God
except philosophically." Brother Tomas also observed
that Spinoza and Prado were "happy to be atheists" but
that "they regretted the absence of the charity that they
used to receive from the synagogue." This last point is
not entirely accurate, since it was only Prado who had
received financial support from the Jewish community
(Nadler, *Spinoza: A Life*, 136).

113. *According to the testimony that was later gathered:*
The concern of the synagogue's leaders to round up
incriminating testimony allegedly provoked Prado's
acidic remark, "[T]hese little Jews want to establish an
Inquisition in Amsterdam." (Nadler, *Spinoza: A Life*, 143).

114. *"Thorns [in Spanish, Espinos] are they that, in the* Fields
[Prados] of impiety": Nadler, *Spinoza: A Life*, 145.

115. *a Jewish man armed with a knife:* Bayle reports that the
      incident occurred just outside a theater and suggests
      that the assault accelerated Spinoza's decision to break
      with the Jewish community (Bayle, 282). Colerus
      tells essentially the same story, but he asserts that
      the attack occurred outside a synagogue (Colerus,
      10), and he adds the detail of Spinoza keeping the
      torn coat all his life. There is no obvious mention of
      such a coat in either of the two inventories that were
      made of the philosopher's possessions upon his death
      (Freudenthal, 154–56 and 158–65).

115. *two young members of the Nation approached Bento:*
      Lucas, the source for this incident, reports that the
      young men asked Spinoza three questions: "Has God
      a body? Are there any Angels? Is the soul immortal?"
      To the first question, Spinoza replied that "there
      is nothing objectionable in believing that God is a
      body"—which in retrospect seems a rough prelude to
      his eventual equation of God and nature. To the second
      question, Spinoza responded that angels are not "real
      and permanent substances" but "mere phantoms" and
      that there is no doctrinal necessity to believe in them.
      To the third question, Spinoza answered that the Bible
      provides no proof whatsoever of the soul's immortality.
      At that point, already feeling uneasy about the young
      men's motives, Spinoza put an abrupt end to the
      conversation (Wolf, 44–47).

116. *"only philosophically":* I base these words on Brother
      Tomas's report to the Inquisition (Nadler, *Spinoza: A
      Life*, 136).

117. *he "knew the gravity" of Rabbi Mortera's threats:*
      Spinoza's response to Rabbi Mortera is recorded by
      Lucas (Wolf, 50).

Chapter 12: Excommunication

119. *The weekly wage of a skilled worker:* Schama, 617.

121. *"The Lords of the* ma'amad*":* Nadler, *Spinoza: A Life*,
      120–21.

122. *"with the 613 precepts":* This number appears in the Talmud, the sprawling masterpiece of rabbinic Judaism that was completed around 500 C.E. In the Middle Ages, Maimonides and other rabbinic scholars produced itemized lists of the commandments in line with the Talmudic total.

122. *"Joshua banned Jericho . . . Elisha cursed the boys":* Joshua 6 and 2 Kings 2:23–25. The subsequent series of curses consists of various biblical verses.

124. *not the only one to use these puns:* In 1666, seventeen years before de Barrios wrote his history, Abraham Pereyra wrote, "What is this world except barren ground, a field full of thistles and thorns [*espinos*], a green meadow [*prado*] full of venomous serpents" (Nadler, *Spinoza: A Life*, 146).

126. *"Since Daniel de Prado has been convicted by various witnesses":* Nadler, *Spinoza: A Life*, 144.

129. *"All the better":* Lucas is the source of this quotation (Wolf, 51).

PART ONE: *A Pioneering Outcast*

Chapter 13: Lenses and the New Science

134. *the young man fell deeply in love:* Among the early sources only Colerus mentions this episode, and most scholars dismiss it as fictitious. Aside from the lack of corroborating evidence, Spinoza's frosty rationality seems at odds with romance. In the *Ethics*, he advises against romantic love because it leaves one at the mercy of forces beyond one's own control. It is tempting to interpret this aversion to romance as the result of an early disappointment, but Nadler points out that Clara Maria would have been only thirteen years old in 1657, when Spinoza's supposed rival, then eighteen, began attending Van den Enden's school. Spinoza was then already twenty-five, somewhat old, even at that time, for a match with someone so young (*Spinoza: A Life*, 108).

135. *The invention of the microscope and telescope:* A lovely story tells how the telescope might have been invented around the year 1600. Two children were playing in

the shop of a spectacle-maker in Middelburg, a city in the southwestern part of the Dutch Republic. Quite by chance, the children put two lenses together, one concave and one convex. When they gazed through them in the direction of the town church, they delightedly found that the distant weathervane on the church's roof looked unusually enlarged (Boorstin, 314).

136. *"a free hand yields safer and better results than any machine"*: Letter 32 (*Spinoza: Complete Works*, 850).

137. *four elements—earth, air, fire, and water:* Each element was believed to correspond to one of the four humors, or fluids, that ran through the body: air to blood, water to phlegm, fire to yellow bile, and earth to black bile; eventually, these humors were associated, respectively, with the heart, brain, liver, and spleen. Each person's body contained a unique mixture of each of the humors, and the predominance of a specific humor was associated with a particular personality type. A person in whom blood predominated was courageous and optimistic, while a person in whom yellow bile predominated was irritable and easily angered. Problems resulted from an imbalance in the mixture. A person unable to control his or her emotions, for instance, suffered from too much blood, and the obvious cure was bloodletting. These traditional views have left their imprint on our vocabulary. "Sanguine," which comes from *sanguis*, the Latin word for blood, means "optimistic," and "bilious," stemming from the word "bile," means "bad-tempered."

138. *a fifth element, ether:* The word "quintessence," which refers to the best or purest example of a thing, derives from this belief in a fifth ("quint") essence.

Chapter 14: The Cartesian Revolution

152. *our senses sometimes lead us to the wrong conclusions:* Descartes's misgivings went deeper than the commonplace awareness that we frequently misinterpret sensory data. We all know, for instance, that our eyes might trick us into believing that a mountain is closer than it really is. But Descartes

was actually calling into doubt *all* knowledge gained through our senses. He pointed out, for example, that the things we dream seem perfectly real as we sleep, but when we wake up, we realize they were only imaginary. Since there is no foolproof way to distinguish between our waking and sleeping states, we can never be entirely sure that we are awake, and we therefore have no solid proof that what we perceive actually exists.

158. *the philosophy department, at least, became a stronghold of Cartesian thought:* The philosophy department avoided confrontations with the authorities by steering clear of religious issues. Professors with Cartesian sympathies drew a line between reason and faith and claimed that each is independent of the other. The job of reason, they claimed, is to determine what is true and what is not true, while the job of faith is to help people lead good, moral lives. These two different disciplines properly belonged to two different departments: reason to the department of philosophy, and faith to the department of theology. Spinoza later drew much the same distinction in his treatment of the Bible in the *Theological-Political Treatise*. The Bible, he claimed, is true and valuable as a guide to moral conduct, but it cannot and does not teach any truths about the natural world, which is the proper domain of science.

159. *"[T]here are some atheists in Amsterdam; many of them are Cartesians":* Nadler, *Spinoza: A Life*, 158.

Chapter 15: Launching a Written Philosophy

163. *many of them in direct opposition to Descartes:* A major difference between the two philosophers concerns the number of substances in the world. While Descartes believed that there are two substances—mind and body—Spinoza believed that mind and body are part of a single, all-embracing substance. I say a bit more about this issue in Part II, Chapter 5 of this book.

168. *special praise from his astronomer friend Christiaan Huygens:* Huygens's respect for the lenses was not

quite matched by his respect for the individual who crafted them. His letters contain disdainful references to Spinoza as "the Jew of Voorburg" and "our Israelite" (Nadler, *Spinoza: A Life*, 183). These references are highly ironic since both the Jewish community and Spinoza himself had rejected his identity as a Jew.

Chapter 16: Radical Views of Nature and God

174. *"I believe that a triangle, if it could speak":* Letter 56 (*Spinoza: Complete Works*, 904).

174. *"[T]o ascribe to God those attributes":* Letter 23 (*Spinoza: Complete Works*, 833).

176. *"Furthermore conceive, if you please":* Letter 58 (*Spinoza: Complete Works*, 909).

176. *"Wicked men are no less to be feared":* Letter 58 (*Spinoza: Complete Works*, 910).

179. *"[A]theists are usually inordinately fond of honours and riches":* Letter 43 (*Spinoza: Complete Works*, 878). The assumption that atheists live evil lifestyles was so strong that Bayle, after praising Spinoza's honest and amiable personality, makes the following comment: "This is strange, but after all it is not a more surprising thing than to see men live an ill life, though they be fully persuaded of the truth of the gospel" (Bayle, 283).

Chapter 17: Caution and Cartesian Lessons

184. *"So, to make an end of all this":* Short Treatise on God, Man, and His Well-Being (*Spinoza: Complete Works*, 102).

188. *"[W]e then spoke about such important topics as through a lattice-window":* Letter 1 (*Spinoza: Complete Works*, 760).

188. *"Indeed, there is no one who is more of a trouble to me":* Letter 9 (*Spinoza: Complete Works*, 781).

194. to work for *"the benefit of all men"* and *"to spread the truth":* Letter 15 (*Spinoza: Complete Works*, 800).

Chapter 18: Plagues of Body and Mind

196.   *he drew his own face on the body of a fisherman:* We know
of this sketch from Colerus, who had the assurance
of Spinoza's final landlord, Hendrik van der Spyck,
that the face was that of the philosopher. The figure's
pose was apparently the same as the one commonly
seen in depictions of Masaniello, or Tommaso Aniello,
a young fisherman who in July 1647 led a popular
revolt against Spanish rule in Naples. Although the
revolt was quashed within a few days and the rebel's
head was presented to the Spanish viceroy as a trophy,
Masaniello lived on in the popular imagination as a
heroic freedom fighter.

Stewart (p. 97) makes the interesting suggestion
that when Spinoza drew his own face on Masaniello's
body, he might have been thinking of himself, too,
as a kind of revolutionary, a philosophical freedom
fighter. Unfortunately, none of Spinoza's drawings,
which Colerus tantalizingly describes as having "in my
hands," have made their way to us today.

197.   *"It caused me no little sorrow and anxiety, though that has
much diminished":* Letter 17 (*Spinoza: Complete Works,*
802–3). Spinoza's approach to misfortune was deeply
influenced by Stoicism, a philosophical movement that
arose in Athens during the early third century BCE and
waned only with the spread of Christianity centuries
later. According to Stoicism, the ideal way of life is that
of the sage, the individual who recognizes the necessity
of all things and is therefore unshaken by misfortune
or the turbulent concerns that plague most people.
Today we use the English word "stoic" to describe
an individual who can endure hardships without
complaining.

197.   *"For my part, of all things that are not under my control"*
.... *"I gathered . . . that you are deeply devoted to truth":*
Letter 19 (*Spinoza: Complete Works,* 807).

199.   *The knowledge of God and Religion, defended against the
Outrages of Atheists:* Nadler, *Spinoza: A Life,* 214.

200.   *"And little wonder, since I wish to continue steadfast in the
belief":* Letter 20 (*Spinoza: Complete Works,* 811).

200. *"I see that we disagree not only in the conclusions to be drawn by a chain of reasoning"*: Letter 21 (*Spinoza: Complete Works*, 822).

Chapter 19: Political Upheavals and the Ethics

205. *"For my part"* . . . *"I let everyone go his own way"*: Letter 30 (*Spinoza: Complete Works*, 844).

209. *"just as from the nature of a triangle"*: *Ethics*, Part I, Scholium to Proposition 17 (*Spinoza: Complete Works*, 844).

210. *"Deus, sive natura"*: *Ethics*, Part IV, Preface (*Spinoza: Complete Works*, 321).

210. *"The order and connection of ideas"*: *Ethics*, Part II, Proposition 7 (*Spinoza: Complete Works*, 247).

210. *"a circle existing in Nature and the idea of the existing circle"*: *Ethics*, Part II, Scholium to Proposition 7 (*Spinoza: Complete Works*, 247).

211. *"I shall consider human actions and appetites"*: *Ethics*, Preface to Part III (*Spinoza: Complete Works*, 278). Earlier in the same preface, Spinoza anticipates that readers who "prefer to abuse or deride the emotions and actions of men rather than to understand them" will be surprised by the attempt "to bring logical reasoning to bear on what they proclaim is opposed to reason, and is vain, absurd, and horrifying." Spinoza believed, in other words, that his contemporaries would consider his subject matter—the defective human passions—beneath the dignity of his approach: the pristinely rational deductive process of geometry. Times have certainly changed. If Spinoza were writing today, he might well have to address readers who consider his approach—the coldly inflexible laws of geometry—beneath the dignity of his subject matter: the incomparably rich singularity of each person's emotions and behavior.

212. *What is within our power, however, is the ability to engage in self-reliant actions*: Whether Spinoza's stoic approach to the passions is practical or desirable is a significant

question. Reducing the impact of outside forces on our lives means giving up a great deal of what most of us value—including romantic love (*Ethics*, Part IV, Scholium to Proposition 20, *Spinoza: Complete Works*, 373). Most people, however, are willing to risk the perils of love for the opportunity to forge a deep emotional connection with another human being. Spinoza's pristine, well-ordered universe can be a rather cold place.

Chapter 20: Surges of Religious Unreason

216. *"a man who mocks all religions"*: Nadler, *Spinoza: A Life*, 203.

221. *the Jews of Amsterdam were especially prone to believe:* An additional cause of excitement among Amsterdam's Jews had to do with recent discoveries in the New World. Rabbi Menasseh ben Israel, one of the major rabbis of the Amsterdam community, had concluded in the 1640s that a group of native people in what is now called South America were descendants of one of the Lost Tribes of Israel—Israelites whose traces had disappeared after the fall of the biblical Kingdom of Israel. The idea bore messianic significance: Jewish tradition had long foretold that Jews would be scattered throughout the world before the messiah's arrival, and now, against all odds, Jews had seemingly been discovered in the New World.

221. *many Christians, who eagerly awaited their own messiah:* The year 1666, which Zevi had pinpointed for the redemption, was highly suggestive to many Christians. Chapter 13 of Revelation refers to 666 as "the number of the beast" and "the number of a man," and many Christians linked the number to Christ's Second Coming.

Chapter 21: The *Theological-Political Treatise*

228. *"I hold that the method of interpreting Scripture is no different"*: Theological-Political Treatise, Chapter 7 (*Spinoza: Complete Works*, 457).

232. *On the flip side of the coin:* The idea that the government holds power over the public expression of religion is likely to perplex people accustomed to a more complete American-style separation of church and state. But Spinoza believed that the intense and wasteful rivalry between religious and secular authorities in the Dutch Republic could be avoided only when a single and unambiguous body held all the power—and he was entirely unwilling for that body to be the religious establishment, which he considered manipulative and power-hungry. Spinoza certainly did not want to see a government forcing its recalcitrant citizens to attend church or follow specific religious practices.

     Nonetheless, it is unclear exactly where Spinoza set the dividing line between appropriate involvement and unacceptable interference on the part of the government. What would Spinoza say, for instance, about the efforts of some governments today to ban religious circumcision? What would he say about attempts to outlaw religious articles of clothing, such as headscarves or skullcaps, in public? If such a ban were acceptable, would it include a cross or crucifix worn around one's neck? The boundary between private and public expressions of religion is not always easy to determine.

233. *"real disturbers of peace":* Theological-Political Treatise, Chapter 20 (*Spinoza: Complete Works*, 571).

Chapter 22: Urgent Reasons to Publish

236. *Spinoza was on the opposite side of the conflict:* Spinoza enthusiastically supported De Witt's efforts to ensure a decisive English defeat. Early in the war Spinoza complained that the Dutch "want to be too wise and far-sighted" and were therefore not acting with appropriate aggression (Letter 28, *Spinoza: Complete Works*, 841). It is heartening that Spinoza and Oldenburg managed to communicate respectfully despite their clashing loyalties.

238. *a "marvelous affair"* . . . *"in Scripture, something that is certain and that agrees with reason":* Nadler, *Spinoza: A Life*, 265–66. Israel quotes several other provocative

definitions. Koerbagh defines "heresy," for instance, as "an abuse of power" by churchmen who claim authority that does not belong to them, and he labels "Reformed Religion" a misnomer, since the supposed reform perpetuated the failings of the Catholic Church instead of promoting a "rational religion based on wisdom, truth, and reason" (Israel, 191–92).

Chapter 23: The Furious Public Response

247. *"profane"* . . . *"blasphemous"* . . . *"monstrosities"* . . . *"obscenities"*: These quotations, as well as the ones in the next two paragraphs, appear in Nadler, *A Book Forged in Hell*, 222–25.

248. *"the increase of cry-aloud-to-heaven transgressions"*: Nadler, *A Book Forged in Hell*, 227. Meyer's book, *Philosophy as the Interpreter of Holy Scripture*, was just as inflammatory as Spinoza's, and some people even believed that Spinoza had written it. Meyer's argument is that reason, not faith or religious authority, must be our guide to understanding the Bible. This is the case because the Bible conveys truth, and reason is the only way for us to understand what is true. When reason tells us, for instance, that God cannot have a body because bodies cannot be perfect, infinite, and eternal—as God must be—then we must read biblical passages referring to God's body figuratively, not literally.

249. *"atheist"* . . . *"a godless document"*: Nadler, *A Book Forged in Hell*, 231. A comment made by Thomas Hobbes demonstrates just how thoroughly the *Treatise* rocked the intellectual world of the time. Hobbes, an English contemporary of Spinoza's and one of the most controversial figures of the age, had been labeled an atheist for his assertively secular approach to government and religion. But even Hobbes was taken aback by the *Treatise*, which, he said, "cut through him a bar's length, for he durst not write so boldly" (Nadler, *Spinoza: A Life*, 295–96).

250. *The Truth of the Christian Religion*: Nadler, *A Book Forged in Hell*, 232.

251.   *"I think I have not strayed far from the truth"*: Letter 42 (*Spinoza: Complete Works*, 878).

251.   *"I can hardly bring myself to answer that man's letter"*: Letter 43 (*Spinoza: Complete Works*, 878).

252.   *"his excellency did not want to see him pass his threshold"*: Nadler, *Spinoza: A Life*, 256. Ironically, critics of De Witt denounced him as Spinoza's accomplice, claiming that it was only through De Witt's official protection and support that Spinoza had been able to publish the *Treatise*. Perhaps they had heard the same rumors as Lucas, who reported that Spinoza lived on a pension that he inherited from De Witt's estate (Wolf, 61). There seems to be no truth to these claims. De Witt, despite his Cartesian sympathies and liberal tendencies, was just as horrified by Spinoza as most people of the period.

252.   *"Forged in hell by the apostate Jew"*: Nadler, *A Book Forged in Hell*, 231.

Chapter 24: True Freedom's Gory End

256.   *"I shall obey, but now the De Witts are dead men"*: Nadler, *Spinoza: A Life*, 306.

256.   *The night after the murders, the sickened Spinoza prepared a sign:* Our knowledge of this incident comes from Leibniz, who reports that he heard the story directly from Spinoza during their meeting in 1676 (Freudenthal, 201).

259.   *"stupid Cartesians"*: Letter 68 (*Spinoza: Complete Works*, 935).

Chapter 25: Quiet Amidst the Storm

262.   *"ought to be buried forever in an eternal oblivion"*: Nadler, *A Book Forged in Hell*, 234.

262.   *"From the little that I then read of it"*: Letter 5 (*Spinoza: Complete Works*, 892).

262. *His needs were few:* It is Colerus who reports Spinoza's refusal to accept the full sum from De Vries as well as the lovely details about Spinoza's simplicity and warmth that I present in the next few paragraphs (Colerus, 37–45). "It is scarce credible," the biographer enthuses, "how sober and frugal he was all the time." Colerus also highlights Spinoza's "sweet and easy" conversation, his care never to do "an unbecoming thing," and his "very courteous and obliging" manner. Spinoza must have been a most appealing man to win such praise from someone so hostile to his philosophy.

265. *they were integral to the supernatural religious order:* Since God was also part of this supernatural realm, casting doubt on the existence of any supernatural creature meant casting doubt on the existence of God. It is therefore no surprise that in *A Flower Garden Composed of All Kinds of Loveliness*, some of Koerbagh's most fiercely condemned definitions had to do with supernatural creatures. Koerbagh insisted that "angel" was really "bastard Greek" for a word originally designating nothing more than a human messenger, and he dismissed Satan and demons, along with supernatural activities such as sorcery, witchcraft, possession, exorcism, and divination, as just so many falsehoods concocted to scare and manipulate the ignorant masses (Israel, 191–92).

266. *"I am surprised that those who have seen naked spirits":* Letter 54 (*Spinoza: Complete Works*, 898).

266. *"You will not find elsewhere a Prince more favourably disposed":* Letter 47 (*Spinoza: Complete Works*, 886).

267. *"I do not know within what limits the freedom to philosophise must be confined":* Letter 48 (*Spinoza: Complete Works*, 887).

270. *"I'll go outside, and I'll go straight to them":* Colerus, 49.

Chapter 26: Discouraging Events

274. *The joyous gala continued for eight days:* The celebration's length adhered to the biblical models of the desert Tabernacle and Solomon's Temple, whose

dedications both lasted eight days. Another eight-day celebration took place during the Maccabean Revolt in the second century BCE, when the Second Temple was rededicated, giving rise to the eight-day holiday of Hanukkah. The adherence to biblical models is suggestive. To the first- and second-generation survivors of the Spanish and Portuguese Inquisitions, the public dedication of a magnificent new synagogue must surely have seemed a triumph of almost biblical proportions.

277. *A letter that arrived during that period:* Letter 67 (*Spinoza: Complete Works*, 921–29).

278. *Spinoza finally agreed to write back:* Letter 76 (*Spinoza: Complete Works*, 947–51).

281. *"remove prejudices which have been conceived against it":* Letter 68 (*Spinoza: Complete Works*, 936).

282. *"I have taken great care not to deride, bewail, or execrate human actions": Political Treatise,* Chapter 1 (*Spinoza: Complete Works*, 681).

Chapter 27: Personal Encounters

285. *One day she lingered longer than necessary in Spinoza's room:* My depiction of this scene is based on Colerus, who presumably heard about the incident directly from Ida van der Spyck (Colerus, 41–42).

287. *Spinoza's visitor was a young German man named Gottfried Wilhelm Leibniz:* I am especially indebted to Matthew Stewart's *The Courtier and the Heretic* for my account of this encounter and my discussion of its significance.

289. *treated the "intolerably impudent" work "as it deserves" . . . sorrow that "such a learned man has, as it seems, sunk so low":* Nadler, *Spinoza: A Life,* 301.

289. *"celebrated doctor and profound philosopher":* Letter 45 (*Spinoza: Complete Works*, 884).

289. *"As far as I can judge from his letter":* Letter 76 (*Spinoza: Complete Works*, 941).

290. *"When one . . . compares one's own small talents with those of a Leibniz"*: Stewart, 12.

293. *God freely chose to create the particular world that we inhabit . . . the "best of all possible worlds"*: This idea appears primarily in Leibniz's *Theodicy*, which was first published in 1710. The work introduced not only the famous words "the best of all possible worlds" but also the term "theodicy," which refers to a defense of God's goodness and omnipotence despite the evil that we perceive in the world. Today, many people know the expression "the best of all possible worlds" through Voltaire, the eighteenth-century philosopher whose satirical masterpiece *Candide* viciously mocked Leibniz's optimism.

295. *what Spinoza dismissed in the* Ethics *as "a kingdom within a kingdom"*: *Ethics*, Preface to Part III (*Spinoza: Complete Works*, 277).

295. *"You know that I once went a little too far"*: Stewart, 15.

296. *Spinoza's motives, Leibniz acknowledged, were just as worthy as he considered his own to be:* The quoted words of praise appear in Stewart, 198–99. Leibniz, like Colerus, admired Spinoza as a person but felt a deep aversion to his philosophy.

Chapter 28: Death and Its Aftermath

299. *a "free man thinks of death least of all things"*: *Ethics*, Part IV, Proposition 67 (*Spinoza: Complete Works*, 355).

299. *"would say sometimes to the other lodgers that he was like the serpent"*: Colerus, 38–39.

301. *One wintry Saturday:* The details of Spinoza's last days, the funeral arrangements, and Rebecca's claim to the property are related by Colerus (82–92), who also takes great care to deny the hearsay that swirled around the philosopher's death—either that Spinoza ultimately embraced God or that he barred clergymen from approaching his deathbed. These rumors involved wishful thinking on all sides (Israel, 295–301). The idea of a last-minute repentance appealed to people

so convinced of God's existence that they could not
fathom a dying man's persistence in denying it,
while the idea that the dying Spinoza refused to see
a minister appealed to radical thinkers who did not
want to imagine their hero ultimately succumbing
to religious superstition. Ironically, this latter notion
pleased many religious people, too. Some relished
the thought that Spinoza had willfully missed his last
opportunity to avoid hell, and others took pleasure
in thinking that religion is so true and strong that
even a hardened atheist like Spinoza recognized his
risk of succumbing, and therefore needed to keep all
churchmen away.

303. *refined his Latin:* Spinoza had always relied on his good
friends to edit his Latin, a language in which he had
never felt entirely at home. Even Dutch, the language
of Spinoza's day-to-day affairs after his break with the
Jewish community, never felt as comfortable to him
as the Portuguese of his childhood. In his first letter
to Blijenbergh, Spinoza, writing in Dutch, confessed
his discomfort: "I would have preferred to write in the
language in which I was brought up; I might perhaps
express my thoughts better. But please excuse this, and
correct the mistakes yourself. . . ." (Letter 19, *Spinoza:
Complete Works,* 810).

304. *"This bookseller assured me":* Israel, 289–90.

Epilogue

308. *the English political thinker John Locke:* Locke (1632–
1704) moved to Amsterdam in 1683 and circulated
for five years among people sympathetic to Spinoza's
ideas. Strong evidence of Spinoza's influence appears
throughout the Englishman's work, including the
following passage: "It is not the diversity of opinions
(which cannot be avoided), but the refusal of toleration
to those that are of different opinions (which might
have been granted), that has produced all the bustles
and wars that have been in the Christian world upon
account of religion. The heads and leaders of the
Church, moved by avarice and insatiable desire of
dominion, making use of the immoderate ambition of

magistrates and the credulous superstition of the giddy
multitude, have incensed and animated them against
those that dissent from themselves . . ." (John Locke,
"A Letter Concerning Toleration," in *Treatise of Civil
Government and a Letter Concerning Toleration*, Charles
L. Sherman, ed. [New York: Irvington, 1979], 219).

309.   *Johann Wolfgang von Goethe in Germany:* Goethe
       (1749–1832), one of the greatest German writers of all
       time, describes in his autobiography the enormous
       impact of Spinoza on his life and work: "After
       looking through the world in vain, to find a means of
       development for my strange nature, I at last fell upon
       the *Ethics* of this philosopher. Of what I read out of the
       work and of what I read into it, I can give no account.
       Enough that I found in it a sedative for my passions, and
       that a free, wide view over the sensible and moral world,
       seemed to open before me." (A.J.W. Morrison, trans.,
       *The Auto-Biography of Goethe: Truth and Poetry: From My
       Own Life*, vol. 2 [London: George Bell, 1881], 26).

309.   *George Eliot in England:* Mary Ann Evans (1819–1880),
       a major writer of the Victorian period, composed the
       first known English translation of the *Ethics*. The
       influence of the *Ethics* on her writing is so apparent
       that some people have viewed her fiction as a literary
       adaptation of Spinoza's philosophy. Eliot's novels
       present a deterministic universe in which characters
       find freedom and happiness by subduing their
       passions and recognizing that they are just one small
       part of a larger scheme.

309.   *"I believe in Spinoza's God":* "Einstein Believes in
       'Spinoza's God,'" *New York Times*, April 25, 1929,
       http://query.nytimes.com/mem/archive/pdf?res=F10B
       1EFC3E54167A93C7AB178FD85F4D8285F9.

Note on the Sources

TO GET TO KNOW SPINOZA, THE BEST THING TO DO—
and often the most difficult undertaking—is to read
his own writings. I used *Spinoza: Complete Works*,
edited by Michael L. Morgan, with translations by
Samuel Shirley (Indianapolis: Hackett, 2002).

Spinoza: Complete Works includes all of
Spinoza's surviving correspondence. These letters
provide a wealth of information about Spinoza's
life and a far more intimate view of him than
his philosophical treatises can provide. Most of
the letters, however, are forever lost to us. After
Spinoza's death, his friends respected his wishes
and destroyed all correspondence they did not
consider relevant to his philosophical thinking.

Fortunately for us, Spinoza generated a great
deal of interest both during and immediately after
his lifetime, and two biographies appeared shortly

after his death. One was written by Jean Maximilian Lucas, a Protestant refugee who had fled persecution in France and made his home in Holland. Lucas knew Spinoza personally, and his great admiration for the philosopher is apparent in the biography he began writing in 1677. The second early biography was written by a Lutheran minister, Johan Köhler, now usually called by his Latinized name, Johannes Colerus. At the end of the seventeenth century, Colerus lived in The Hague, where he rented the same widow's rooms in which Spinoza had himself once lived. Since Colerus also served as the minister of the Van der Spycks' church, he was able to hear from two sets of landlords about their famous former tenant. Colerus also took advantage of the opportunity to interview other people in The Hague connected with Spinoza. But Colerus was no admirer, and his biography, published in 1705, exhibits quite a bit of hostility toward its subject.

Lucas wrote his biography in French, and a French translation of Colerus's original Dutch manuscript appeared in 1706. I consulted both of these French works in *Vies de Spinoza* (Paris: Editions Allia, 2002), along with English translations. For Lucas, I used an English translation by A. Wolf entitled *The Oldest Biography of Spinoza* (Port Washington and London: Kennikat Press, 1927), and for Colerus, I used an English version that appeared in 1706 and is readily available in facsimile: *The Life of Benedict de Spinosa. Written by John Colerus, . . . Done out of French* (Gale ECCO, Print Editions, 2010). Because the original English version of Colerus contains many archaic spellings and turns of phrase, I used my own translations from the French whenever I quoted from his work. Nonetheless, page numbers in my notes refer to the original English translation so that readers can more easily consult Colerus's biography themselves.

Another early source about Spinoza's life is Pierre Bayle's *Historical and Critical Dictionary*, which first appeared in French in 1697. The *Historical and Critical Dictionary* is one of the first examples of what we would now call an encyclopedia, and it was one of the most widely read books in Europe in the 1700s. The work's very long entry on Spinoza focuses mostly on philosophical matters, but it also includes some information about Spinoza's life. It seems likely that some of Bayle's sources were Spinoza's friends and acquaintances. Bayle, like Lucas, was a French Protestant who had found refuge in Holland—but unlike Lucas, Bayle was decidedly unfriendly to Spinoza. I consulted Bayle's work in French at http://www.spinozaetnous. org/telechargement/Bayle_Spinoza.pdf. The article is also available in an English translation in *An Historical and Critical Dictionary, Selected and*

Abridged from the Great Work of Peter Bayle, vol. 3
(London: Hunt and Clarke, 1826), 271–340. Page
numbers in my notes refer to this edition, which
is available online at https://archive.org/details/
anhistoricaland01baylgoog.

A major aid to Spinoza scholars is an anthology
of primary source material compiled by Jacob
Freudenthal in *Die Lebensgeschichte Spinoza's in
Quellenschriften, Urkunden und Nichtamtlichen
Nachrichten* (Leipzig: Verlag Von Veit, 1899),
available online at *https://archive.org/details/
dielebensgeschicoofreu*. Most of the texts are
translated into German, but a few are included in
French. I found the collection useful for material I
could not find elsewhere, such as the inventories of
Spinoza's belongings after his death.

Evaluating what is true and untrue in the
early accounts of Spinoza's life is not a simple
matter. For one thing, what counted as truth for
biographers and historians who lived at that time
is not necessarily what would count as truth today.
In the seventeenth and eighteenth centuries,
unsubstantiated hearsay and rumor were quite
likely to be reported as historical fact. The problem
is further complicated by the very pronounced
opinions that Lucas, Colerus, and Bayle had about
Spinoza. An excellent example of this problem is the
episode of brilliant little Bento passing his father's

test with the dishonest old woman. On the one hand, this episode sounds a lot like one of those fictitious stories often told about historical figures we idolize, and it is no surprise that this story appears only in the biography written by the admiring Lucas. On the other hand, Lucas was a personal friend of Spinoza's, and it is quite possible that Lucas heard that story directly from Spinoza himself. Another example is Spinoza being attacked by a fellow Jew as he left the synagogue, an episode that appears in Colerus's account (and with a slight variation in setting— to the outside of a theater—in Bayle's account as well). The episode so conveniently suits Colerus's generally sneering attitude toward Jews and Judaism that it may well be fictitious. On the other hand, Colerus insists that he had the story directly from the Van der Spycks, who themselves claimed to have had it directly from Spinoza.

For the most part, I have decided to include these sorts of stories despite their sometimes questionable nature, and I have generally chosen not to interrupt the flow of my narrative to discuss whether or not they are true. I have taken this approach not only because I believe these stories add color to my account but also because they have become part of the lore surrounding Spinoza. Even contemporary scholars who reject these stories tend not to pass over them in silence but to take the time to acknowledge their existence. While I may have taken some liberty with the truth in including these questionable narratives, I have not exercised that liberty to the point of presenting stories or scenes of my own invention. All of the stories and scenes I depict are grounded in one or another of the sources on Spinoza's life.

Another liberty I have taken concerns Spinoza's inner turmoil in the years before his *cherem*. Because we do not have anything that Spinoza wrote before his mid-twenties, we cannot know exactly what he was thinking when he was younger. The *cherem* declaration provides little help, since it refers only vaguely to Spinoza's "evil opinions and acts," "hateful heresies," and "monstrous deeds." But in my narrative, I felt that I needed some kind of bridge between Spinoza as the model schoolboy and Spinoza as the heretical outcast. I did not, however, invent any of the thoughts I put into Spinoza's head. All of the questions, doubts, and ideas raised by my young adult Spinoza appear in his later writings. Although this retrospective reading of Spinoza violates strict academic standards, I feel justified for several reasons. For one thing, Spinoza's early biographers mention his teenage years as the time his doubts first began to coalesce, and for another, Spinoza was an amazingly consistent thinker throughout his life. And based on my own experience as a teacher, I have no trouble believing that a thoughtful teenager is already taking significant steps toward the ideas that will inform his or her adulthood.

In any case, this book is certainly not meant to present the definitive word on Spinoza but only to provide a basic introduction to a very important thinker. Ultimately I hope that this work will inspire at least some readers to find out more about Spinoza or about other great philosophers. The study is rich and rewarding, and it promises a deeper understanding of where we have been and who we are today.

In addition to the sources I have already mentioned, the following works have helped to shape my presentation of Spinoza and his period:

Ben-Sasson, H.H., ed. *A History of the Jewish People.* Cambridge: Harvard University Press, 1976.

Boorstin, Daniel J. *The Discoverers: A History of Man's Search to Know His World and Himself.* New York: Vintage, 1983.

Goldstein, Rebecca Newberger. *Betraying Spinoza: The Renegade Jew Who Gave Us Modernity.* New York, Schocken: 2006.

Israel, Jonathan I. *Radical Enlightenment: Philosophy and the Making of Modernity 1650–1750.* New York: Oxford University Press, 2001.

Nadler, Steven. *A Book Forged in Hell: Spinoza's Scandalous Treatise and the Birth of the Secular Age.* Princeton: Princeton University Press, 2011.

————. *Spinoza: A Life.* New York: Cambridge University Press, 1999.

————*Spinoza's Ethics: An Introduction*. New York: Cambridge University Press, 2006.

————*Spinoza's Heresy: Immortality and the Jewish Mind*. New York: Oxford University Press, 2001.

Roth, Cecil. *A History of the Marranos*. Philadelphia: Jewish Publication Society, 1932.

Schama, Simon. *The Embarrassment of Riches: An Interpretation of Dutch Culture in the Dutch Golden Age*. New York: Vintage, 1987.

Stewart, Matthew. *The Courtier and the Heretic: Leibniz, Spinoza, and the Fate of God in the Modern World*. New York: Norton, 2006.

Twersky, Isadore, ed. *A Maimonides Reader*. New York: Behrman House, 1972.

Willis, F. Roy. *Western Civilization: An Urban Perspective*. Vol. 1, *From the Rise of Athens through the Seventeenth Century*. Lexington, MA: D.C. Heath, 1973.

Glossary

A note on pronunciation: ḥ = a guttural sound, similar to the "j" in Spanish
For terms relating to the Jewish tradition, I have used the Hebrew pronunciation rather than the Anglicized one.

action: as Spinoza defined it, an emotion or behavior that is self-sufficient in that it depends on the use of one's reason rather than on forces beyond one's control; actions, unlike passions, generate a healthy, expansive sense of the self

anthropomorphism: the assigning of human traits to something that is not human; in an anthropomorphic view of God, which both Maimonides and Spinoza derided, God is conceived as a kind of superman

attribute: in Spinoza's philosophy, an essential characteristic of substance; although the number of attributes is infinite, the only two we are capable of grasping are thought and extension

bar mitzvah: (bar meets-VAH) a person obligated to keep all the laws of Judaism; traditionally, boys who have reached the age of thirteen

bima: (bee-MAH) raised platform in the synagogue from which officiants lead prayers and chant readings from the Torah; Spinoza's *cherem* was announced from the *bima* in the Portuguese synagogue

caute: (COW-tay) the Latin word for "caution" that appeared on Spinoza's seal, a reminder that radical views should not be shared indiscriminately

chachamim: (ḥah-ḥah-MEEM) religious authorities of the Portuguese Jewish community

cherem: (ḥEH-rem) excommunication from the Jewish community over perceived violations of religious law, usually intended as a temporary corrective but especially harsh in Spinoza's case

Collegiants: members of a Protestant group that held Sunday meetings, or "colleges," for joint prayer and study; Collegiants recognized the Bible as the only source of religious authority and held that individuals could believe and practice as they chose

crypto-Jews: forced converts to Christianity who secretly maintained Jewish practices; these individuals were major targets of the Inquisition, which considered crypto-Judaism a form of heresy

Deus, sive natura: (DAY–oos SEE-vay nah-TYOO-rah) Latin for "God, or nature," an encapsulation of Spinoza's position that God is identical to substance, not a supreme, external force that acts upon the world; because of its explosive content, the phrase appeared only in the Latin version of the *Ethics*

Dutch Golden Age: the period from the late 1500s until the *Rampjaar* in 1672, when the Dutch Republic became one of the world's most prominent economic powers and many people in the Republic enjoyed great prosperity

empiricism: the idea, in contrast to rationalism, that we arrive at knowledge through the evidence that our senses provide; empiricism is at the heart of the scientific method, which tests hypotheses through experiment and observation

Escamoth: (ehs-kah-MOTE) the register of community resolutions and regulations kept by the Portuguese Jewish community; the text of Spinoza's *cherem* appears in one of the volumes

extension: the physical taking up of space, which according to Spinoza is one of the two attributes of substance that we know; the modes of extension are physical bodies

ghetto: in the history of Jewish communities, the small area of a city, often locked at night, where Jews were allowed to live; the first ghetto was established in Venice in the early 1500s and lasted almost three hundred years

heresy: the refusal to believe or act as one's religion demands; heresy was the violation that the Inquisition sought to stamp out

Inquisition: the centuries-long, organized attempt by the Catholic Church to find, put on trial, and punish any Christian suspected of heresy; in Spain and Portugal, the Inquisition's major targets were Jews who had become New Christians

ma'amad: (mah-ah-MAHD) the Portuguese synagogue's governing committee

marranos: (muh-RAH-nohs) an insulting designation for New Christians who were suspected of secretly practicing Judaism; the term may come from the Spanish word for "swine"

mezuza: (m'zoo-ZAH; plural *mezuzot*) a parchment containing handwritten biblical texts that is traditionally attached to a doorpost, often in a decorative case

mode: as Spinoza defined it, a specific expression of an attribute of substance; all physical bodies are modes of the attribute extension, and all ideas are modes of the attribute thought

Moors: Muslims in the Iberian peninsula, who were forced into baptism or exile by the Christians who had conquered their land; like crypto-Jews, many Moors converted but secretly remained faithful to their religion

la Nação: (lah NAH-sah-oh) Portuguese for "the Nation," the name that Portuguese Jews gave to their own community

natura naturans: (nah-TYOO-rah nah-tyoo-RAHNS) Latin for "naturing nature," which Spinoza conceived as the self-causing activity of nature—essentially the interconnected system of laws applying in all places and at all times

natura naturata: (nah-TYOO-rah nah-tyoo-RAH-tah) Latin for "natured nature," which Spinoza conceived as the passive product of the causal chains of *natura naturans*— essentially, the sum total of the animal, mineral, and vegetable entities we usually call "nature"

necessity: in Spinoza's thought, the idea that nothing can be other than it is—including human action—because everything is the result of long chains of cause and effect

New Christians: Jews or Muslims who had converted to Christianity, usually because they had been coerced to do so; New Christians were often suspected of heresy and targeted by the Inquisition

oligarchy: rule by a small and privileged group of powerful people; in the Dutch Republic, these people were generally prominent merchants

passion: as Spinoza defined it, an emotion or behavior that is generated by things over which we have no control; unlike actions, passions destroy our sense of well-being

predikanten: (pray-dee-KAHN-ten) ministers of the Dutch Reformed Church, who often found themselves at odds with the merchant oligarchy

prime mover: (in Latin, *primum mobile*) the original and eternal source of motion that is in itself unmoved or unaffected by anything else, often identified with God by religious thinkers

Purim: (POO-reem) springtime Jewish holiday that commemorates the salvation of Persian Jews as recorded in the biblical Book of Esther

Rampjaar: (RAHMP-yahr) the "Disaster Year" of 1672, when the Dutch Republic was under the attack of England, France, and the German states of Cologne and Münster; also in that year, the lynching of the De Witts put a definitive end to True Freedom

rationalism: the idea that accurate knowledge comes through the exercise of reason and logic, not through sensory experience as empiricism claims

rubi: (ROO-bee) a variant of "rabbi," the term that young Bento and his classmates would have used to refer to their teacher at school

sanbenito: (sahn-beh-NEE-toh) a tunic that bore symbols of specific sins and was part of the penitential costume that convicted heretics were forced to wear on their way to execution

seder: (SEH-dehr) evening feast held at the beginning of Passover to commemorate the biblical story of the Exodus, when the Hebrew slaves were liberated from their Egyptian oppressors

shofar: (shoh-FAHR) ram's horn associated with God's judgment, traditionally blown in the synagogue on Rosh Hashanah, the Jewish new year

siddur: (see-DOOR) traditional Jewish prayer book

stadtholder: (STAT-hohl-der) Dutch hereditary head of state

sub specie aeternitatis: (soob SPEH-kee-ay eye-tehr-nee-TAH-tis) Latin for "under the aspect of eternity," a perspective from which one views one's life as just one tiny element within the grand scheme of nature

substance: the primal stuff of the universe, the thing that needs nothing else to exist and that, according to Spinoza, has an infinite number of attributes; Spinoza believed that there was only one substance, and he identified it with God

Sukkot: (soo-KOHT) Jewish Feast of Tabernacles, celebrated in the fall, when people move out of their homes to live or at least to dine in temporary huts

tallit: (tah-LEET; plural *tallitot*) a rectangular piece of fabric with fringes, traditionally worn by Jewish men as a prayer shawl

tefillin: (t'fee-LEEN) small leather boxes containing slips of parchment inscribed with biblical passages, traditionally used by Jewish men during weekday prayers; one box is tied to the forehead and a second box is tied to an arm

theodicy: a defense of God's goodness and omnipotence despite the evil that we perceive in the world; Leibniz coined the word as the title of the book he wrote on the subject

thought: according to Spinoza, one of the two attributes of substance that we know; the modes of thought are ideas

Torah: (toh-RAH) the scroll containing the Five Books of Moses that is publicly read in the synagogue; more broadly, the term can refer to all the books of the Jewish Bible as well as to the totality of Jewish teaching and learning

True Freedom: the period when the Dutch Republic was led by Grand Pensionary Johan de Witt, who coined the term; under True Freedom, the Republic opposed monarchy, supported the merchant oligarchy, and maintained generally tolerant policies

Tulip Mania: the Dutch frenzy over buying and selling tulip bulbs during the 1630s, when the prices for certain varieties reached absurdly high levels; the inevitable market crash brought financial ruin to many investors

Index

actions, 211–212, 282, 326–327, 345
   See also passions
afterlife, 71–79, *76f*, 101, 175
   See also soul, immortality of
Alvares, Anthony and Gabriel, 90–91, 112
Amsterdam
   bookstores in, 32, 104, *106f*, 161
   diverse population of, 84–85
   intolerance in, 78, 81
   Jewish community of, 3–6, 16, *24f*, 25–42, *31f, 35f, 36f*, 219–221. *See also* Nation, the (la Naçāo) (Jewish community of Amsterdam)
   Jewish refugees, arrival of, 18–20
   Jewish refugees in, 313
   new synagogue and, 274–275
   population growth in, 46–48
   poverty and crime in, 55
   response to *Theological-Political Treatise* in, 247
   shipbuilding in, *47f*
   tolerance in, 7, 18, 21–23, 87
   wealth in, 48–54

Anglo-Dutch war, 203–205, 216, 236, 254, 328
Aniello, Tommaso. *See* Masaniello
anthropomorphism, 99–100, 345
Aristotle, 100
atheism, 114–116, 159, 179–180, 249, 251, 318, 324
attributes, 210–211, 345
authority
   of the Bible, 66, 104, 113, 199–200, 296, 319
   of government, 230–232, 328
   of rabbis, 65–66, 78, 124, 126
   religious, 144, 329
   Spinoza's impact on, 309

Balling, Pieter, 161, 194, 197
Bank of Amsterdam, 49
bar mitzvah, 39, 345
Bayle, Pierre, 320, 324, 339–341
Bento. *See* Spinoza, Benedict de
"best of all possible worlds," 293, 333
Beth Israel, *35f*
Bible
   authority of, 66, 145, 199–200, 296, 319
   authorship of, 61–64, 113, 228, 315